"Sr. Genevieve's storytelling and personal reflections illuminate unexpected nuggets of wisdom found in the living Word. As I read this book, I knew I was reading the words of a wise woman of prayer! This is a book I will turn to again and again for inspiration."

—Becky Eldredge, author of *The Inner Chapel* and
Busy Lives & Restless Souls

"Sr. Genevieve Glen invites us to read with her in the lamplight, to be enlightened by a 'small, warm, and friendly flame,' which is the divine Presence. She uses poetry, history, and her own life experience to give us a new way of looking at familiar biblical stories and personalities. What shines out under this lamplight is Sr. Genevieve's prayerful reflection from many years of living with the word of God."

—Jerome Kodell, OSB, former abbot of Subiaco Abbey,
Subiaco, Arkansas

"Sr. Genevieve Glen, OSB, offers us a book penned with lyrical language that invites compelling inquiry. I've read books that leave me with a felt connection to the writer. This book is the first one that left me with the impression that the author actually knows me, the reader."

—Mary Margaret Funk, OSB, Our Lady of Grace
Monastery, Beech Grove, Indiana

D1267470

By Lamplight

A Book of Biblical Reflections

Genevieve Glen, OSB

A *Give Us This Day* Book

LITURGICAL PRESS
Collegeville, Minnesota

www.litpress.org

A *Give Us This Day* Book
published by Liturgical Press

Cover design by Amy Marc

Cover art courtesy of Getty Images

Versions of many of these essays originally appeared in *Give Us This Day* (Collegeville, MN: Liturgical Press), www.giveusthisday.org. Used with permission.

1	2	3	4	5	6	7	8	9

Library of Congress Cataloging-in-Publication Data

Names: Glen, Genevieve, author.
Title: By lamplight : a book of biblical reflections / Genevieve Glen, OSB.
Description: Collegeville, Minnesota : Liturgical Press, [2021] | Includes bibliographical references. | Summary: "Reflections on familiar images of Word and Light, from Nazareth to Emmaus, Psalms to Beatitudes, Advent to Pentecost, through characters, stories, and prayers"— Provided by publisher.
Identifiers: LCCN 2021025714 (print) | LCCN 2021025715 (ebook) | ISBN 9780814666104 (paperback) | ISBN 9780814666364 (epub) | ISBN 9780814666364 (pdf)
Subjects: LCSH: Meditations. | Catholic Church—Doctrines—Meditations.
Classification: LCC BX2182.3 G54 2021 (print) | LCC BX2182.3 (ebook) | DDC 242—dc23
LC record available at https://lccn.loc.gov/2021025714
LC ebook record available at https://lccn.loc.gov/2021025715

Acknowledgments

This book would never have happened without the encouragement and inspiration of Abbess Maria-Michael, OSB, and the nuns of my Benedictine community, the Abbey of St. Walburga. And it would never have reached print without the patient encouragement and editorial skill of Peter Dwyer, director of Liturgical Press, and Mary Stommes, editor of *Give Us This Day*, both long-valued friends, and the newfound gem of an editor, Amy Ekeh, director of Little Rock Scripture Study, and without the dedication and skill of the staff of Liturgical Press.

Contents

Introduction: Reading by Lamplight

Abraham Lincoln became my hero when I was nine years old—not, alas, because of the Gettysburg Address or the Emancipation Proclamation, but because I was chosen to act the role in a class play in honor of Lincoln's birthday. The choice was not made because of my thespian talents. It was because I was the tallest kid in the class.

All I remember about this dramatic debut was the paper stovepipe hat and the fake beard and the protests of the boys who, I am happy to report, soon outgrew me. But by that time my family had moved to a colder climate and into a house with a real fireplace. Always an avid reader, I discovered the joy of lying on the floor in front of a good fire, reading a book. When my father protested about eyestrain, I called upon Lincoln's example for vindication. While boning up to play the role, I had learned that, being poor, Lincoln read by the fire at night because he had to work during the day. This did not stop him from becoming president, giving the Gettysburg Address, or issuing the Emancipation Proclamation. So I continued to read by the fire.

Many years later I lived in Houston for some time. NASA's mission control was only a few miles down the road, and all eyes were on space. One night, by some quirk of an unusually cooperative atmosphere, the skies above us, typically masked by city lights, were carpeted with stars. I went outside to see. As I looked at all that faraway white beauty, I was suddenly struck by fear and loneliness. There I was, a tiny, insignificant speck of humanity, totally overwhelmed by that vast, impersonal glory, starlit but untenanted—or so it seemed. Unseen mercy supplied a line from the book of Revelation: "The city had no need of sun or moon to shine on it, for the glory of

God gave it light, and its lamp was the Lamb" (21:23). And the Lamb was a person I knew and loved. My loneliness and disorientation slipped away. That immense white field of lights was funneled down to a single light by which I could see and walk unafraid.

Lamplight, I came to realize, was firelight when Revelation was written. With a lamp, one could take comfort in reading by a small, warm, and friendly flame. And this flame was the Presence who is "the light of the world" (John 8:12), God's burning love made flesh. A line from the Psalms has been my guide ever since: "Your word is a lamp for my feet, / and a light for my path" (119:105). It is the light by which I have read the passages that have inspired the reflections in this book.

Reading is never a solitary act, even when no one else can be seen in the room. I am deeply grateful to all those, visible and invisible, who have held the lamp for me down the years so that I could read more clearly. And to Abraham Lincoln, who first taught me that however dark the night may be, you can always read by the light of the fire.

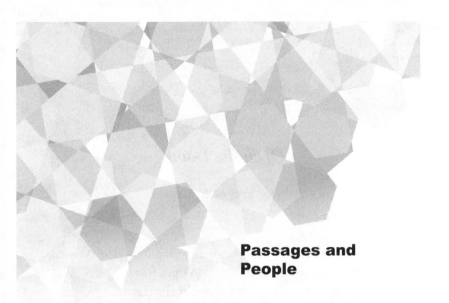

Passages and People

Open the Door

Come, let us walk in the light of the LORD.

—*Isaiah 2:5*

When I wake up in the early morning dark, the door of my room is outlined faintly in light from the hall. Out there are morning coffee, notes about the day on the white board on the way to the coffee pot, information about what liturgy we're celebrating today, and, of course, the rest of my community. Out there are the good things that go a long way toward making me who I am.

"Come," says the prophet Isaiah. In other words, we have to leave where we are and go somewhere else. He's inviting us to get up from whatever darkness we might be inhabiting right now and go out there, to the house of God, from which flows the one essential light: the light of the Lord. Without that light, we risk wandering around in the dark all day, even when kitchen lights, office lights, warehouse lights, school lights, and a plethora of other lights shine around us everywhere we go. Of course, we know something Isaiah could only hope for: the essential light is not a bulb flipped on by a switch, but Jesus Christ, a person, "the light of the world" (John 8:12). For us, he is the light that leads us through and beyond every dark place. We don't always see or recognize him among all those other bright and familiar lights. But God has given us a book of instructions to help us recognize which light is which and to guide us to the one that will lead us even through the ultimate darkness of death. We know this book as the Bible: "Your word is a lamp for my feet, / and a light for my path" (Ps 119:105).

Of course, this path lets us go in two directions: out and in. The prophet invites us to go out—to leave where we are and go somewhere we aren't yet. But the path on which the Word of God sets our feet can also take us *in*. We live in Christ, the Light, so we can expect to find that light in the depths of our lives, the depths of our minds and hearts. However, "in" may be the last place we want to go to seek it. When we turn inward, we may have to face the dark places of our own hearts. We all have them, and we don't usually want to go there. But if we do, we may see a door outlined in light. And we may hear someone knocking at it, and a voice saying, "Here I am! I stand at the door knocking! Let me in so we can sit down together for a while!" (see Rev 3:20). And when we open the door, we will find that Christ is there, in our deepest center, flooding our interior darkness with light. That flood of light banishes the darkness, warms the cold places, and gives us the energy to embrace life as it comes to us today.

Come. Take up the invitation. Dare to walk out of the dark— whether it's loneliness, emptiness, fear, anger, or some other misery. Open the door that is in you. The Light that you meet there can be blinding. You may find yourself disoriented for a bit, but just stay for a while on the threshold till the eyes of your heart adjust. Then go wherever the Light shines. You might be surprised by where the path leads.

The Measure of Love

Whatever form it may take, the most important "good work" of Christians is love. "It is characteristic of the greatest love to give itself as food," said St. Albert the Great (1200–1280), speaking of God's love given in Jesus Christ in the Eucharist. "Oh, good!" we may say, "This is not something *I* have to do!" But it is! Jesus himself said, "As I have loved you, so you also should love one another" (John 13:34). If Jesus gives us his love as food, then, so must we do for one another.

Let's think for a moment about what kind of food we have to give. Remember what good, nourishing food does for us. It keeps us as fully alive as we can be, helping us not only to breathe in and out, but to think, feel, reach out to the world around us with curiosity and concern, exercise our creativity, seek truth and beauty, and reach for the stars. In other words, food makes it possible for us to do all those things that characterize us human beings at our best. It keeps us healthy. It gives us strength. It makes us grow. So necessary is a good diet to human well-being that Christian charity consistently finds all sorts of ways to feed the hungry, so that even the poorest might benefit in every way from Jesus' mission: "I came so that they might have life and have it more abundantly" (John 10:10).

Now let's think about what poor nutrition does to us—not *for* us, mind you, but *to* us. Whether it is poverty or affluence that deprives us of a balanced diet rich in the foods the human body really needs, we are diminished. Our energy is quickly depleted. Our minds grow sluggish as our bodies grow tired. We become a door open to disease. The circle of our interest can dwindle to the size of a plate of food—either food we long for but cannot afford, or food we crave and consume without limit. In every way, we are impoverished.

"By their fruits you will know them" (Matt 7:16). Healthy love, like a healthy diet, bears fruit in healthy human beings. God's love, of course, gives us life in every way possible. Our love for one another might be more modest, but it rewards both givers and receivers with a fullness of life that is otherwise out of reach. Remember, for example, the person who loved you enough to stand by you as you failed again and again at something that mattered—tottering across the living room for the first time, or passing the test for your driver's license, or getting the job you really wanted—and gave you the courage to keep trying until you succeeded. Maybe you never even noticed how much pain your failures cost the one who loved you; you only saw and heard their faith in you: "You tried. I love you. Give it another try! I'm behind you!" Remember the person who pushed and pulled you through school until you suddenly woke up and discovered you *liked* learning. Think of the person who mentored and encouraged you in the work you had chosen, even when you were ready to quit. Remember a time when you loved someone enough to let them walk away into their own future, leaving you behind. Real love costs, of course. But it also gives us strength. It makes us grow beyond the place where we started.

Unhealthy love, on the other hand, saps and shrinks us. Possessive love, for example, consumes us in order to feed another person's "love." It deprives us of the strength and freedom to *become*. Demanding love sucks us dry: "If you loved me, you would . . ." Hypercritical love shrinks our confidence to nothing: "You know you can't bake a cake! You always mess it up!" Love like this is merely self-love in disguise—and sometimes the mask is very thin!

You will notice that not much has been said about feelings. St. Thomas Aquinas (1225–1274) said that to love is to will the good of others. He did not say that to love is to feel warmly toward them 24/7. Good feelings fuel and are fueled by love, but building decisions on feelings is building on sand. Love that relies entirely on feelings will collapse in the next storm. Feelings must mature into commitment, choice, and action if love is to stand firm. Warm feelings might draw us to a person—spouse, parent, child, sibling, friend, neighbor—but only commitment will keep us there when the warmth has cooled under the pressure of illness, work, financial stress, anger, or hurt. Noble feelings might move us toward the cross, but they rarely survive the pain of the nails. Action is the ultimate measure of love: What will I do (or refrain from doing) for the sake of those I love—without begrudging the cost to myself?

Jesus shows us the only real answer: "[O]n the night he was handed over, [he] took bread, and, after he had given thanks, broke it and said, 'This is my body that is for you. Do this in remembrance of me'" (1 Cor 11:23-24).

Stay at Home

So said St. Benedict of Nursia in his monastic Rule. He meant it literally for his monastic followers: *Stay at home.* In fact he translated it into a vow of stability, which means putting down roots in one place.

But Benedict is much more than a lawmaker. He has also become a teacher of wisdom for people in all walks of life. His center is Christ, and his perennial source is the Bible. Beyond its literal meaning, his call to "stay at home" teaches us all something about reading and praying the Scriptures, inside or outside monasteries.

Jesus identified "home" as his Word: "If you make my word your home, you will be true disciples" (John 8:31; *The Jerusalem Bible*). In Jesus' day, the disciples lived where he did. For us today, home is where our roots are. Whatever our actual memories of home are, happy or troubled, most of us long for a home where we can go for comfort, strengthening, and inner clarity. It is a matter not of geographical place but of a personal center, or what Scripture calls "the heart." This home is what we make of it by experience, by choice, and by habit. This is the home Jesus urges us to make of his Word.

Jesus may have been a builder, like most carpenters of his day, so it is likely not by chance that he talks about home building. Remember the lesson about building a house on rock, not sand (Matt 7:24-27)? "Rock" is a much-used biblical image to describe God and God's Word as our shelter and strength. St. Paul applies it to Jesus (1 Cor 10:1-4), God's Word-made-flesh (John 1:14). So, as we live in and with the Word recorded in Scripture, we are making our own the home that Christ has built for us and shares with us (Ps 127:1). And we learn that it is a house of many rooms (John 14:2).

Some prayer guides list Bible passages for particular needs like trust, grieving, or doubt. But as we turn again and again to this passage or that, we are in fact making our own personal list of which rooms we go to often and why. They become home to us, a home to which we return to start the day, take a quiet break, or round out the evening. These biblical verses are the place where we gradually take root and from which we grow, like the fruitful tree in Psalm 1 whose leaves never wither. The habit of spending time there offers all of us, in any walk of life, the stability that St. Benedict urged.

And we never go home alone. God's Word is always an invitation to engage in conversational exchange, whether verbal or silent. And often enough, the conversation brings us into the company of people within the biblical stories—Moses, Miriam, David, Mary, Peter, and all the others we have come to know. Being at home in the Word allows us solitude when we need it but always offers good company. It's a comforting, nourishing, and transforming place to be.

So, says St. Benedict, the wise teacher: At least sometimes, stay at home!

Blessed Are They Who Mourn

Blessings poured out on those who have done something deserving of reward make gospel sense. Our desire for a happy ending earned is satisfied when we hear in the Beatitudes that those who have chosen to be poor in spirit end up with a kingdom—and the kingdom of heaven, no less (Matt 5:1-12)! It makes sense to us that those who have chosen meekness over a self-assertive grab for power turn out to be the ones who gain the land they refused to take by force. We understand why the merciful are themselves shown mercy. But those who mourn? What is praiseworthy about mourning?

The classical answer, provided in treatises on the Beatitudes like that of St. Leo the Great (ca. 400–461), is not the fact that these mourners grieved but *what* they grieved: their sins. Repentance is certainly urged and commended throughout the Scriptures, but somehow it seems to sit uneasily among more obvious beatitudes like hungering and thirsting for justice or devoting oneself to peacemaking. These others all seem to carry some sense of doing good for others. Of course, in St. Paul's view, whatever makes one person holier strengthens the sanctity of the whole Body of believers, so in that sense, mourning one's sins benefits everyone if the mourning is followed by a change of behavior (1 Cor 12:26). But that bit of sophisticated theological reasoning is out of character with the simple directness of Jesus' Beatitudes, either in Matthew's version (5:1-12) or Luke's (6:20-22).

Perhaps we might look differently, then, at what these mourners grieve. The fact is that ordinarily we do not mourn what we have not loved and lost. The very word "mourners" conjures up concrete images of family and friends weeping beside a grave. It may be that the mourners are given their place among the "blessed" precisely because they have loved enough to grieve people they have lost—friends, family, fellow citizens—to whatever forces tore them away—death, separation, antagonism, or worst of all, the cold chill of indifference.

When we look at the Gospels, we discover that Jesus himself is twice described as mourning. He wept at the grave of his friend Lazarus, beloved and lost to him in death, before raising him again (John 11:35). He also wept over Jerusalem (Luke 19:41), lost to him through a long history of refusing the love that so longed to gather up and restore what sin had been scattering since the Tower of Babel (Gen 11:1-9).

Finding Jesus among the blessed company of mourners opens a wider vista on all eight of the beatitudes he proposes. Not only in mourning but also in embracing poverty of spirit, in choosing meekness over power and violence, in hungering and thirsting for righteousness, in showing mercy, in becoming single-hearted, and in making peace, Jesus' disciples then and now have not merely embraced abstract virtues. They have mirrored Christ, as people made in God's image must do (Gen 1:26; 2 Cor 3:18; 1 John 3:2). And in every case, they have done so by expressing the love he taught in action. For example, those who have chosen poverty of spirit have aligned themselves with the Christ who made himself poor in order to make us rich (2 Cor 8:9). Those who are meek mirror the Christ who chose to take to extremes his own commandment to love one's enemies and turn the other cheek when wronged. Meekness, he demonstrates, is acting not out of weakness but out of the strength of a love that works to transform enemies rather than destroy them (Matt 5:38-41). The blessed who have chosen to offer mercy to others become like him who used his last breath to beg the Father to forgive those who had sent him to the cross on which he hung dying (Luke 23:34).

And the mourners? They have opened their hearts wide to accept their own pain, born of their love, in company with Christ. Then they have turned their attention away from themselves to offer comfort to others.

The Beatitudes can be read as Jesus' self-portrait. All those who put them into practice, mourners included, are living mirrors of Christ in every age.

God's Vocabulary

G od has quite a dynamic vocabulary. Take, for example, a line from the succinct poetry of the creation story in Genesis 1: "Let the earth bring forth every kind of living creature: tame animals, crawling things, and every kind of wild animal" (v. 24). At our monastery, "every kind of wild animal" includes the bear seated in the wild plum tree behind the house, devouring all the fruit, ignoring an audience of nuns and dogs and the groans of overburdened branches. It includes the curious marmots lined up at low-set chapel windows to watch our liturgical calisthenics as we stand, sit, and kneel. It includes the two abandoned fox cubs happily growing up in our farmyard and serving as self-appointed greeters to guests arriving in the parking lot. These are just a glimpse of the rich array of wild animals populating our planet over millennia. And the rich array of words that spoke them into being.

Take, as another example, the fruits of that sentence spoken as the conclusion of the creation story: "Let us make human beings in our image . . ." (Gen 1:26). The book of Revelation envisions these beings growing into "a great multitude, which no one could count, from every nation, race, people, and tongue" (7:9). Just imagine: a gathering of countless words first spoken by God and then taken up by these "hearers of the Word" as the vocabulary they would embody and live (see Jas 1:22).

But this vocabulary is a choice.

On the one hand, Jesus lists a sample of the phrases adopted and lived by this multitude: *poor in spirit, merciful, clean of heart*, and the rest of the Beatitudes (Matt 5:1-12). We could add others from the list describing love in 1 Corinthians 13: *patient, kind, courteous, humble.* Or the list of fruits of the Holy Spirit in Galatians 5:22: *joy, peace, faithfulness.*

On the other hand, there are different words than God's that are fighting to be selected and lived, words spoken by the whispers of evil uttered through undiscerning teachers or mentors, or through calculating demagogues: *richest, most powerful, proudest.*

Choose we must, and choose we do. And blessed are those wise enough to consult God's ultimate Word of Love, made flesh in Christ. British mystic and poet Carryll Houselander believed this to be a Word with too many syllables to count. "We are only," she said, "syllables of the perfect Word." And mirroring Christ, God's first Word, in our own limited ways, we ourselves may become not a single word of many syllables— that is a communion of which we, in our finitude, are not capable—but a rather a complex collection of words fitted together as best we can. As we live and choose, we add these other words to the words that first defined us. Word by word, choice by choice, we slowly write into being the full language we will become.

A caution: there are words we never celebrate, words like *wicked, liar,* and *predator.* The Scriptures tell stories of those who choose not to relinquish words like these, words that distort and destroy our humanity. As a lover of language, I lament when beautiful words are degraded into the coarse, vulgar, pornographic, or blasphemous. How much more reason to grieve the loss of those who choose them as their only reality. All we can do is place our hope in God's great counter-words of love—*conversion* and *forgiveness*—and pray that those who have become the twisted, broken vocabulary spoken by evil will allow these dehumanizing words to be redeemed and rewritten.

Let us remember that the God who speaks reality into being is still writing the book of the living kept by the Lamb (Rev 13:8). Let us work, love, and pray for one another so that when God at last puts down the pen, the vocabulary list complete, every human name will appear on those pages.

And the last words God writes will be: *Amen! Alleluia!*

Jesus' Not-So-Hidden Years

ustom has encouraged us to see Jesus' life on earth as a diptych: the first panel, only vaguely filled in, is his dramatic early childhood, followed by the so-called "hidden years" of which the Gospels tell no stories; the second panel, much clearer, portrays his public ministry. So seething with activity are his public years after a long privacy that we tend to forget that Jesus lived his life as a whole, as we all do.

When he left Nazareth for the wilderness of Judea where John was baptizing, and the desert where he wrestled with the Tempter, and, finally, the towns and roads of Galilee and Judea and beyond, he did not arrive there as a wide-eyed stranger seeing the world for the first time. Jesus had at least thirty years behind him, most of them probably spent in Nazareth and its environs. He was already the mature adult that experience and choice had made him.

Reading as most of us do in English, we imagine Jesus to have spent those "hidden" years doing carpentry for his fellow villagers. However, the Greek word translated as "carpenter" (Mark 6:3) can also mean "builder" in a broader sense. Scholars have ventured to propose that Jesus and Joseph might have traveled beyond Nazareth to work in places besides the familiar village carpenter shop so beloved of religious art. The Gospels do not say. But wherever Jesus worked and whatever he worked at, he did more during those years than earn a living while he bided his time till his public ministry would begin. Rather, he gathered in what life in a Galilean village and its environs had to teach him about the world he had come to redeem.

The nuclear family that many cultures within the United States take as the norm would have been rare in Palestine. We can surmise that Jesus grew up as part of a typical extended family that included not only Mary and Joseph but all the other relatives who play cameo roles in the Gospels: his aunt, Mary's sister, for example (John 19:25), and the various "brothers" and "sisters" (Mark 3:31; 6:3), kinship words that could refer to siblings or cousins. No doubt there were others who are not mentioned because they played no major role in the unfolding of his public life.

He would also have had plenty of neighbors to play with when he was young and to talk with when he grew older. He was apparently no solitary dreamer but a relative and neighbor so unremarkable that the townsfolk couldn't take in the startling claim he later made to be the one who fulfilled Isaiah's prophecy, the one Spirit-anointed to "bring glad tidings to the poor. / . . . to proclaim liberty to captives / and recovery of

sight to the blind, / to let the oppressed go free, / and to proclaim a year acceptable to the Lord" (Luke 4:18-19; Isa 61:1-2).
To them, he was the local carpenter, the son of Mary and Joseph, the boy next door. What did he know of these activities
that more than hinted of the promised messiah? But Jesus
would have had most of thirty years to have known the poor,
to have met people captive to destructive thoughts and habits,
to have encountered blind villagers, and to have seen people
oppressed by life's sometimes overwhelming forces. And he
no doubt lived cheek by jowl among them with the same compassion he showed them all through his public years.

We know very few concrete details of Jesus' growing up, but
we do know a good bit about what he observed, heard, thought
about, and probed for images of the reign of God—images he
would later flesh out in his public ministry. He paid attention
to the field anemones we know better as the "lilies of the field."
He noticed birds, both as wild beneficiaries of God's providence and as small, helpless victims of hunters and merchants.
He had an eye for the weather: "Red sky at night, shepherd's
delight, red sky in the morning, shepherd's warning" (or its
Greek equivalent in Luke 12:54-56). He seems to have paid a
good bit of attention to local agriculture. He was familiar with
the cultivation of vines and fig trees. Galilee served as the
breadbasket of Palestine, and Jesus knew all about the sowing,
harvesting, and grinding of wheat for flour, as well as the work
of combining yeast and flour together, kneading the dough,
letting it rise, and baking it in the village ovens.

Jesus also took note of the human landscape in which he
lived. He knew of family squabbles over inheritances. He
would have had no need to invent the parable of the Prodigal
Son from scratch. No doubt he knew a family or two where a
younger son had taken off to sow his wild oats, with unhappy
results. He knew the pitfalls that could bring a wealthy land-

owner to a sorry end. He had heard enough of the fabled
bandits who prowled the Jericho road to give flesh to the parable of the Good Samaritan. And he had obviously observed
with compassion the struggles of the poor to survive, the mis-
eries of lepers, the pain of the blind, deaf, mute, and disabled.
The human foibles, the human suffering, the human tragedies
he met (and retold in memorable stories) during his public
years did not come as news to him when he encountered them.

And, given his habit of withdrawing into solitary prayer
during his ministry, we have to assume that as Jesus prayed,
he mulled over all he learned about the world and its human
inhabitants in communion with the Father and the Spirit. That
experience and that prayer became the very heart of what he
showed and taught about the reign of God, which is God's
goal for us.

God, says the book of Genesis, saw all of creation as good.
But the creation God loved most profoundly seems to have
been, and still is, humanity. Jesus, God's love made flesh, took
seriously the world into which he had been sent, paid attention
to it, understood it. And that long learning and loving and
comprehending did not begin when he first walked onto the
beach near Capernaum announcing that the kingdom of God
was at hand (Mark 1:15).

So, as we reflect on the years of Jesus' public ministry, let us
remember what they grew out of. Let us see the two panels of
the traditional diptych together as the single life of the One
who loved and redeemed it all. As we do, we will come to know
him more deeply. Perhaps with St. Paul we will even come to
say, "I . . . consider everything as a loss because of the su-
preme good of knowing Christ Jesus my Lord" (Phil 3:8).

Knowing grows into loving and serving. Long ago, the old
Baltimore Catechism hit the nail on the head when it taught
us that God made us to know, love, and serve him in this

world. And Jesus' second commandment urges us to know, love, and serve one another too (Matt 22:39).

As our own lives, hidden and public, unfold by the gift of God's creative love, let us endeavor to do just that.

Landscapes of Hope

A sower went out to sow—a common sight in the fertile fields of Galilee. Sowers scattered seed by hand, just as Jesus describes it. The workday was long and hard, the sowing slow. There was no time, and no necessity, to place every grain carefully on arable soil. Working with a rhythm handed down from generation to generation, the sower could best sow by swinging hand and arm in a wide arc while walking with a steady pace that could be sustained for a long time.

The seed fell where it fell—on paths beaten hard by passersby at the field's edge, among rocks that would have consumed too much time and energy to clear, in patches of thorn bushes, but mostly on fruitful ground that always bore a good crop, sun and rain permitting. When the sowing was done, the farmer traded the seed bag for a wooden plow to turn the ground under and bury the grain. Jesus and his hearers would have seen this done countless times, year after year.

Jesus transformed this sowing scene into a parable about the hard work of growing the reign of God, like a field of wheat, among hearers of every sort (Mark 4:1-20). He said that a sower (who was, of course, Jesus himself) sowed the Word, the good news of God's reign. Then he used the landscapes on which the seed fell to describe the hearers. Some, he said, were hard of heart, like the paths beaten solid by passersby (4:4). In the landscapes of the spirit, we all have byways beaten into near stone by the constant march of the thoughts that preoccupy us: *No use talking to her, she never listens. It wasn't my fault. It never is, but he criticizes me anyway. Love my enemies? He's got to be kidding! Doesn't he know what they've done to me? Why should I keep quiet when she's picking on me? I don't have to put up with that kind of treatment! Turn the other cheek? Who really does that?* Over and over, the thoughts repeat on a loop that becomes such a habit of mind that we never question it. No access there for the gospel seed!

As for "rocky ground" (4:5), we have only to take a look at the places where our hearts have hardened into stone. Selfishness has landscaped them into caves and prisons we no longer notice much: *I have a right to take care of myself. Too bad if I shut out my parents—they don't care—or my pastor—he's a hypocrite, don't you see?* Or, *Do you believe that supervisor who told me to go easy on that co-worker who just lost a spouse and was walking around in a fog? We've all got our problems, but we have to get the job done, otherwise no raises!* We may be deafer than we know to all the versions of "love your neighbor as yourself" (Matt 22:39; Mark 12:31; Luke 10:27) that call out to us every day. No room for anyone else in that rock-bound cave of ours!

And briar patches (4:7)? We may indeed listen to the gospel, maybe even make good resolutions about changing our ways after we hear that homily or read that book that seems right on. But inevitably, "worldly anxiety, the lure of riches, and the craving for other things intrude," as Jesus warns (4:19). *I really do think I should give some of my stuff away—I don't use half of it anyway. But I might need one of these things someday. Better hold on to it all.* Or, *I know I should pray, but I'm too worried about my family, the economy, the violence downtown, climate change, and the end of the world to focus on saying those prayers I used to say or reading the Bible—it's out of date anyway, don't you think?* Or, *I really will start spending more time with my family, but first I need to pick up a few more shifts at work. We're doing fine, but I'd feel better if we had a better bottom line.* St. Paul was not far off when he said that not money itself but the love of it is the root of all evils, from hoarding to stealing to shooting up a bank (1 Tim 6:10)! And we are all familiar with the ways those cravings can dominate our lives—from chocolate to another bottle to a designer outfit, a bigger house, or, most dangerous of all, the yearning for more power.

One of the most painful and rarely noted facets of Jesus' explanation of this parable is that it seems to say that whatever our failings—shallow surface, hardness of heart, worries of all sorts—they all have one thing in common. They are incurable. Paths will be paths, rocks will be rocks, briars will be briars till the end of our days, and so it seems that no crops will grow, no matter how patiently or how many times the Sower scatters the Word into our lives.

Parables do rely on worst-case scenarios to get our attention and break through into our thoughts and lives. A parable is a powerful story-telling device that makes us sit up and take notice. But it is never the whole story. An anonymous author of the fifth or sixth century, writing under the pseudonym Macarius (the name of a venerated Egyptian monk of the fourth century), presented the parable of the sower in the light of hope. He wrote that Christ, the real Sower, does not stop when the sowing is done. Rather, he takes up the cross as a plow and uses it to break up all the stubborn landscapes of the heart: hardened habits of thought, dense hearts of stone, and stifled lives entrapped in thorns. His death and resurrection deliver us from the unbreakable hold death seems to have on us, whatever form that death may take, and they bring us out of every tomb we have chosen into the bright light of a new life.

Yes, Jesus has already begun this work. He does not simply look on and see where the seed is going, or sit back and wait for rain and sun to do their work. He cares far less about where the seed falls than about the transformation it can bring about in the landscapes that receive it. And the seed that is God's Word gives life in the most unlikely places. The deepest reason for this is that Christ himself is the one essential seed that falls to the ground (John 12:24) and is plowed under to become the bread that feeds more than just a few thousand on a hill in Galilee (Matt 14:21). He is a wise farmer after all. He knows that one grain alone, even if he is that grain, is not enough. It takes many grains of wheat to make enough flour to be baked into bread to feed all the hungry, including ourselves. He continues to plant his Word and his presence as seeds in our hearts. He continues to cultivate the landscapes of our lives to become fields fertile enough to yield wheat to supply bread for every human spirit that genuinely hungers for the abundant life he promised (John 6:34; 10:10). He takes that heavy plow, the cross, and breaks open ears and hearts hardened against the life-giving Word, opens up stone tombs in which we have chosen to live, and tears away every thornbush, with hands calloused and scarred by the work. We are assured by the voice of God, the harvest owner, speaking through the prophet Isaiah, that the Word that God has sent forth will not return empty but will achieve the end for which that Word—enfleshed in Jesus Christ (John 1:14)—was sent:

Yet just as from the heavens
the rain and snow come down
And do not return there
   till they have watered the earth,
   making it fertile and fruitful,
Giving seed to the one who sows
   and bread to the one who eats,
So shall my word be
   that goes forth from my mouth;
It shall not return to me empty,
   but shall do what pleases me,
   achieving the end for which I sent it. (Isa 55:10-11)

The Gift of a Stone

If your children ask for a loaf of bread, would you give them a stone?

If you wouldn't, asks Jesus, how can you imagine that God would (Matt 7:9-11)? The trouble is that God's gifts of bread sometimes feel like stones! A bad day at the heavenly bakery? Divine meanness? Or simply a confirmation of the widespread suspicion that God is not really on our side after all?

Take out some of those stones you've accumulated over the years in response to your pleas for bread. Take a good look at them. Some will still look and feel as indigestible as stones: heavy, crushing burdens that defy any effort to understand the "why" of the gift. But some of them may look a little bit different now, in the clarifying light cast by distance and experience.

Long ago I had reason to reflect on a difficult home publishing project that my community undertook, we thought, in obedience to God. By a mischievous quirk of Divine Providence, I was assigned to take charge. It was one of *those* projects. From beginning to end, everything that could go wrong did. Equipment suddenly drew lines in the sand and refused to cross them. "I don't do that," said the manuals in very tiny print. "It's not in my job description." Software exercised every form of perversity it could cook up. "You want page numbers *there*? Ha! Dream on!" An essential component dawdled around forever in the mail, thumbing its nose at the calendar on my office wall, which relentlessly announced that our deadline was galloping up with the speed of a Triple Crown winner. The printer suddenly ran out of a consumable we didn't even know it had. Asked *why* the item had run out, it sulked in silence with no information forthcoming except that it would print not one more word until the component was replaced. And we had no replacement on hand.

The project had looked like such a *gift*, I wailed privately to a patient Providence. Why had things unfolded this way? Later, when the project had in fact been completed in good time, contrary to every expectation, I looked back and saw hidden facets of the stone gleaming in the light of a different day. The project had been difficult. It had been stressful. It had cost us sleep and given us headaches. However, it had also taught us a great deal. We had learned the capabilities and limitations of our equipment. We had learned countless lessons about page layout, font sizes, and graphics. We had learned what supplies we needed to keep on hand. We had acquired valuable information about the inner workings of the printer, hidden from unsuspecting operators. And we had, as originally hoped, created a product that could be of service.

The example is very small in the larger scale of things. No one died. No one went bankrupt. No one lost a loved one or a job or a home. No one lost anything, in fact, except a little peace of mind and a bit of sleep.

But it taught me a lesson about some of the stones delivered by the celestial bakery truck. A stone can, in fact, be a very valuable gift. I had wanted a project that would fall into place easily, run smoothly, turn out perfectly, be finished quickly, and stroke my pride in the achievement. What I got was hard work with a steep learning curve that demanded ingenuity, patience, and perseverance—all qualities in which I need endless practice. I got a better understanding of what our equipment could and could not do, and of what *we* could and could not do—a practicum in the kind of realism that recognizes and embraces life as it is rather than life as I want it to be. I got the satisfaction of work decently but not perfectly done by a team of committed people in and outside of the monastery—a good dose of the humility that unseats the Lone Ranger ego from her high horse with a healthy thump. And I got a greater understanding of myself and others—what our unexpected gifts are, what we need, how we can best work individually and together. What I got from this stone, in other words, was a great variety of gifts that nourish over the long haul, rather than the simple eat-it-now loaf of bread I had hoped for.

As I have often explained to God, I hate lab courses. I would so much rather read all the answers and explanations in a book without having to mess with exploding test tubes or spilled chemicals or strange smells in the room. However, as God has often explained to me, the lab of life is a place where we learn from one experiment how to solve a whole host of other problems, some of them seemingly unrelated.

Indeed, from this particular experiment I learned something about coping with other kinds of stones. Among them are experiences more serious than this one: difficult people around me, hardened places in my own heart, and even some of the "hard sayings" of Scripture—like the image of God as a parent who will not give stones when asked for bread, and yet sometimes does. Some of these stones are hard because they are demanding. Some are hard because they seem incomprehensible. Some are hard simply because they are unbearably heavy no matter how we hold them. However, more often than not, these stones come bearing gifts, as this one small pebble in my life did. With a little willingness to listen, a little unhurried attention, and a little persevering patience, we can often learn to crack open the outer stone to discover the bread it conceals.

Life is full of stones—some as small as pebbles on a beach that hurt our feet when we step on them, some as immense as the great stumbling blocks of evil, sin, and death that can cripple our entire selves. And so life requires a lot of stone work. As we read and ponder God's gifts of words, we may find ourselves engaged in wrestling matches with pebbles and stumbling blocks alike, breaking open "hard sayings" in Scripture and hard experiences along the way, in search of their inner nourishment.

Jesus has promised that our heavenly Father will give good gifts to those who ask (Matt 7:11). And so we can trust that God does provide bread—even when it looks like a stone!

Sheep and Goats: Taking Another Look

Jesus' parable of the sheep and the goats (Matt 25:31-46) conjures up wrenching images from a time not so far from our own. Reimagine the scene in more modern terms: The all-powerful judge stands before a milling crowd, no doubt tense and frightened about what is to come. The judge has a clipboard, from which he reads out name after name. As each one stands before him, he consults the clipboard and decrees "Acceptable!" and nods toward a gate to his right, or "Unacceptable!" and nods toward the gate to his left. No recourse is given to pleas or arguments. Off they go—one group to life, the other to death. The judge might wear the uniform of a Nazi soldier or a Soviet Gulag official or the executor of any other tyrant's will. The gates might lead to sections of a concentration camp, a work camp, or a death camp. We have read such stories and shuddered at them.

But Jesus' story in Matthew 25 bears only a superficial resemblance to those scenes of horror. Let's peel back the modern dress. The judge is no soulless martinet standing in judgement before a hapless crowd of conquered victims. Jesus, the storyteller, identifies the judge as Christ come in glory, surrounded by angels and facing all the nations gathered for the final judgement. The "sheep" and "goats," representing the people, are vivid images meant to engage Jesus' listeners, for whom flocks and herds were part of normal life. Rich and poor are there; people of every color and shape are there; monarchs and peasants are there—and you and I and all our families and neighbors are there too.

The criterion for sentencing is not race or politics. The real criterion is how those being judged have treated—or, surprisingly, *not* treated—other people. So unexpected is this standard that those being judged have a hard time grasping it, as, no doubt, did Jesus' hearers. The judgement is absolute: eternal life in God's unending reign or punishment among those who have rejected God altogether. As vivid as the images of sheep and goats, these destinations are most definitely attention-getters.

Now let us go behind the parable itself to discover a deeper reality. The judge, Christ come in glory, is of course none other than Jesus himself—crucified, died, and risen. But long before death or glory, Jesus described himself as the Good Shepherd (John 10:11). This shepherd is no merciless judge. This shepherd goes after every sheep lost from the safety of the flock, as we see him do over and over again in the Gospels.

Behind the figure of the shepherd, we find the prophetic tradition revealing that this shepherd is none other than God—a God who goes to enormous trouble to find the lost and bring them home. Through Ezekiel, for example, God says, "Look! I myself will search for my sheep . . . I will deliver them from every place where they were scattered on the day of dark clouds. . . . In good pastures I will pasture them . . . I myself will pasture my sheep; I myself will give them rest. The lost I will search out, the strays I will bring back, the injured I will bind up, and the sick I will heal" (Ezek 34:11-14). In the Gospel, this same God made flesh in Christ is the shepherd who, in fact, plunges even into the depths of death to bring back the sheep confined there. Here is the shepherd who has comforted generations through Psalm 23, a favorite for all who have been lost, found, and brought home to the house of the Lord.

The Good Shepherd is hardly an unbiased judge. Christ is out to send as many as possible through the gate marked "Life." And that's not a clipboard he's holding—it's the gospel promise of forgiveness for all who provide even the smallest reason for the shepherd judge to stamp their foreheads "pardoned" (see Rev 7:3). Long before the story's final end, this shepherd has willingly followed the flock wherever even the least and worst of them have gone—out into the leper camps, into the isolation of the outcast, down into the valley of the shadow of death—anywhere that those judged unacceptable by their fellow sheep can be found. In order to bring all of us home together, Christ has climbed even the barren rocky hill of his enemies' final judgement, the hill that still bears the memory of the cross. For his very real flock, the shepherd wants only life and has died to provide it.

Along the way the Good Shepherd will not dismiss anyone for the label that someone else has hung around his or her neck: sheep, goat, prodigal, tax collector, prostitute, foreigner, untouchable, useless, deformed, outcast (even scribe or Pharisee!). By the time of his return, no one will have gone through that dark gate marked "Death" except those who have finally refused the shepherd's repeated efforts to bring them home.

That is not to say the judgement is not real. In Ezekiel 34, God-the-Shepherd does warn that the members of the motley flock delivered from dreadful circumstances of every kind will be judged by the way they have treated one another. In both Ezekiel 34 and Matthew 25, however, this final judgement is nothing other than a confirmation that some of us may in the end have chosen our own sorry destination, despite all the Shepherd's efforts to persuade us to turn away from the neglect and destruction we have meted out to our fellow sheep, ways we have stubbornly refused to abandon no matter how great the love we ourselves have received.

Jesus' parable of judgement only summarizes the end of that painful story—and pleads with us to choose life for ourselves by choosing life for others.

Anna

When St. Luke tells the story of Mary and Joseph taking the child Jesus to the Temple to present him to the Lord as prescribed by the law, he assigns a small "walk-on" part to Anna, an elderly widow who had been a fixture in the Jerusalem Temple for many years. The evangelist describes Anna as a woman of unceasing worship, prayer, and fasting. She makes her brief appearance right after Simeon takes the six-week-old Jesus in his arms and blesses God for allowing him to see the promise of salvation fulfilled in this child, whom he describes as "a light for revelation to the Gentiles, / and glory for your people Israel" (2:32). Simeon then warns Mary of conflict and suffering to come. Anna has no such script. A prophetess, she simply gives "thanks to God and [speaks] about the child to all who were awaiting the redemption of Jerusalem" (2:38). Then she disappears back into the holy obscurity from which she came.

Yet Anna still haunts the imagination as an icon of the Godward life to which we are all called. As St. Paul put it to the Thessalonians, "Pray without ceasing. In all circumstances give thanks" (1 Thess 5:17-18), and to the Romans, "Rejoice in hope, endure in affliction, persevere in prayer" (Rom 12:12). Anna had done all of these things for more years than we can imagine, living the whole time in God's company. No wonder she immediately recognized God's startling presence in this one small child brought before the Lord by an ordinary-looking couple from a country village! And no wonder she began immediately to tell everyone about what she had seen, though she was a woman—and an elderly one at that—perhaps easily dismissed as an oddity. Self-consciousness cannot hinder one so saturated with God's presence that she has no concern left over for herself.

Anna's life of unceasing prayer, set free by the discipline of fasting and marked by many years in a sacred setting, is certainly admirable. And yet it hardly seems to qualify her as an icon for those of us who live in ordinary surroundings, fasting a bit when feasible and praying when we can scrounge the time, the quiet, and the solitude in the midst of our busy lives.

But it is easy to underestimate Anna.

First of all, we should not imagine her at prayer in a peaceful environment of holy silence that might make saints of all of us. The Temple was a crowded, noisy place, a hub for pilgrims and tourists, a marketplace for worshippers seeking to buy animals for sacrifice or change their ordinary money for temple coinage to pay for sacrifices and offerings. The Court of the Women, the section of the Temple where Anna spent most of her life, also housed the temple treasury, itself a busy place. Along one wall stood thirteen donation boxes shaped like trumpets where contributors made their donations, all in coins. Large donations dropped in ostentatiously made more noise than small ones, thus summoning up the image of the wealthy donors "trumpeting" their offering. It was there that Jesus pointed out to his disciples the contrast between rich contributors and the widow who offered two small coins, all she had (Luke 21:1-4). No one attempted to hush him because it was normal for people to talk there. This was the environment where Anna would have lived and prayed, perhaps sleeping in one of the small rooms that surrounded the courtyards. She would not have had access to the areas nearer the Holy of Holies because they were not open to women. So her life of constant prayer was nothing like that of people today who spend time in silent prayer in a local parish church or an adoration chapel attached to it. It was, oddly, a marketplace life, despite its Temple context.

Secondly, we should not imagine Anna living in prayerful withdrawal from all the noisy *hoi polloi* around her, refusing to speak to anyone lest she interrupt her conversation with God. A woman of the Temple was necessarily a woman of the covenant—a covenant Jesus echoed when he instructed his listeners to "love your neighbor as yourself" (Lev 19:18; see also Matt 22:39). Women in distress would have come to the Temple's Court of the Women to seek God's help. They would have been grateful for compassion and counsel, and Anna would hardly have ignored them. In both the Jewish and Christian traditions, it has always been customary for the troubled who are seeking God's help and guidance to turn to wise counselors to comfort and advise them. Before the advent of professional spiritual directors, their choice most often fell on people of prayer. Anna would certainly have drawn such seekers.

Besides, in the shifting Temple crowd, people would have had other, more practical needs: mothers looking for lost children, pilgrims suddenly weak with hunger from too zealous a fast, women fleeing abusive kin, destitute beggars dressed in rags that were no longer adequate for winter's cold. Wherever there are crowds of people, there are people in need. After years of life in God's presence, Anna could hardly have failed to notice them as she had noticed the couple from Nazareth with their baby. And she would have known that loving one's neighbor quite often requires very down-to-earth help.

But still, we might object, she did actually live in the Temple—not in a small apartment downtown, or in a home bustling with the comings and goings of family, or crowded into a space with others equally unable to afford better housing. And she never left the Temple to go out shopping or visiting or taking on part-time work. We might imagine that if we lived full-time in the Temple, we too could become people of unceasing prayer and unfailing charity, with the eyes of our hearts open to recognize the Savior in a child.

But we do. Jesus himself is the new and everlasting Temple, the living and enduring replacement for the Temple made of stone (John 2:19-22). The Temple was always understood as God's dwelling place—and by virtue of the incarnation, Christ is that dwelling place in a new and fuller way (John 1:14). Baptized into him, we are always in this new Temple where we "live and move and have our being" (Acts 17:28), as Anna did in the Jerusalem Temple.

Christ urges us to take up our dwelling place in him and, like Anna in the Temple, never leave (Luke 2:37). Here we will be bathed always in his life-giving presence and love even as we share life with others, just as Anna did, for Jesus has promised, "Whoever remains in me and I in [them] will bear much fruit" (John 15:5).

Good News

"The beginning of the gospel of Jesus Christ [the Son of God]."

—*Mark 1:1*

These opening words of Mark's Gospel lead us straight into an empty desert. But for those who know the story of

God's people described in the first books of the Bible, no desert is ever really empty. Sand, rock, and scrub are steeped in the memory of the God who led a motley band of reluctant slaves out of Egypt, through a terrifying passage between walls of water, and into those long desert years between Egypt and the Promised Land. This memory is so strong that the desert—this desert in which the good news of Jesus Christ opens—offers hope that the God of the journey to freedom will reappear after centuries of silence, as promised by the prophets. The desert itself becomes the first of the evangelist Mark's veiled allusions to the God of Israel, all hints that the longed-for Messiah, Jesus, is far more than meets the eye.

But before he appears on the scene we hear a voice offstage repeating the prophetic promise, made not to the waiting people, but to that one who is to come: "Behold, I am sending my messenger ahead of you; he will prepare your way. A voice of one crying out in the desert: 'Prepare the way of the Lord, make straight his paths'" (Mark 1:3; Isa 40:3). The title "Lord" (*adonai* in Hebrew), often substituted for the Holy Name of God, is a second tacit allusion to the real identity of the one whose way must be prepared. And John the Baptist appears, doing just that.

His is an odd preparation, and a dramatic one, if we read all three of the Synoptic Gospels' accounts (Matt 3:1-12; Mark 1:1-8; Luke 3:1-18). The Baptist begins simply by offering a baptism of repentance for the forgiveness of sin. And the people flock to him—all sorts of people—from ordinary folk to religious leaders to tax collectors to soldiers. They empty the city of Jerusalem with their exodus to the river (Mark 1:5). And this is not just any river. This is the Jordan, the river their long-ago ancestors crossed dry-shod to enter the Promised Land, following the ark of the covenant, that forceful symbol of the presence of God (Josh 3:17).

What is most astonishing about this desert scene is that so many are eager to confess their sins publicly and be freed of them, heedless of their reputations. Is it simply the love of a good spectacle that draws them, or is it a deep-felt, perhaps irrational, hope that after centuries of prophetic silence, God's ancient promise of deliverance might now at last be kept?

It is almost as if they hope that John himself is the promised redeemer, come to free them of their burden of wrongdoing and wrong thinking. And, indeed, the religious leaders ask him that very question ("Who are you?"), but he claims that this flood of forgiveness is only preparation for the promised one still to come (John 1:19-28). John is preparing the way, bringing to the fore how badly they all hunger for God to break the long silence and appear among them again.

John's is no gentle persuasion; he offers no soft assurances of love and forgiveness. He stands before them wild and accusatory, marshaling the simple power of words—the power that brought creation into being, a power with which he will clear away, as if with flail and whip, not the people but their illusions. He names their sins so specifically that they cannot dodge behind generalities. His is fire and brimstone preaching, quite literally! Going so far as to call them "a brood of vipers" (Luke 3:7), he demands that they change their ways radically. He offers no consolation to salve their wounded spirits. On the contrary, he promises that the greater emissary still to come will be armed with winnowing fan, axe, and fire (Luke 3:9, 17).

They do not leave. They do not argue. They do not pick up stones to silence him. They go into the water, though they must surely realize from John's warnings that the true Messiah will demand much more of them than a simple bath of repentance.

John gives fierce warning of one armed with blade and fire, Word and Spirit. Mark calls readers to expect one who is far more than the wildest guesses of the crowds on Jordan's banks. The Messiah they both proclaim is disconcerting. We might want to limit ourselves to less disturbing images of the Jesus who treats sufferers kindly, restores dead relatives to those who mourn, and likes children. Those portrayals are all true and all presented in the Gospels. But taken alone, they may fail us in our hour of greatest need. When we find ourselves face-to-face with the real and frightening power of evil, what we most sorely cry out for is the Savior who wields the full might of God. This is the Messiah proclaimed by John and Mark. This is the Messiah who left the Jordan for the desert and later for Calvary, where he defied evil at its most seductive and its most ferocious—and won. This, too, is *our* Savior.

Who?

One day as Jesus was teaching in a house, his mother and brothers showed up outside and asked for him. Deeply engaged with his audience, he asked, "Who are my mother and [my] brothers?" (Mark 3:33). He looked around at his hearers and answered his own question: "Here are my mother and my brothers. [For] whoever does the will of God is my brother and sister and mother" (3:34-35). With these words,

Jesus succeeded in embarrassing generations of believers who have found themselves scrounging around for an explanation that would excuse Jesus' rudeness to his birth family, especially his mother!

Perhaps it would help if we read this little story on two levels—a luxury Jesus' original hearers did not have. Beneath the obvious interchange between Jesus and his audience lies Jesus' actual relationship with Mary. The evangelists do not explore it because they have other news to tell. But think of any relationship you know between two people who love one another deeply and intensely, and have for years. They often seem to be aware of one another's presence nearby no matter what else they may be doing at the time. Twins are a common example of such a relationship, as are couples long married, or family members who share a close tie. If we step back from that puzzling scene as Mark reports it, we may remember that Mary and Jesus spent over thirty years together before he left home to take up his public ministry. We might also recall Luke's account of the conversation between Mary and the angel Gabriel. She—and, at this point, she alone—knew who he really was. And probably something of what it would cost him (1:26-38).

And he, better than anyone else, knew her. When Jesus spoke of those who do the will of his Father, he surely had before his mind's eye the woman outside. Any mother can tell you from experience what it takes to bear and raise a child into adulthood. Her whole body and her whole mind and the whole range of her emotions take a deeply personal part in the process of pregnancy, of giving birth to her child, and of bringing the child up. Mary's reply to the angel's word, "Behold, I am the handmaid of the Lord. May it be done to me according to your word" (Luke 1:38), set in motion the intimate process of receiving God's very Word made flesh into every fiber of her being and every moment of her life from that moment forward. Her openness was all the more profound because she was constrained by none of the self-protective barriers we sin-conditioned human beings put up against the demands of love. Like any good mother, Mary would have known when Jesus skinned his knees, when a neighbor's callous treatment of a playmate pained him, when he came home filled with the glory of the field anemones, the lilies of the field, that he had seen while walking in the Galilean countryside. And surely she would have watched his growing recognition of the work that lay ahead of him as he listened inwardly to the Father's voice in a silence no Gospel reports. And she would have seen the look in his eyes when he had to tell her that his time had come and he must go.

It seems impossible that this mother and this son would not have grown into the kind of unspoken bond that allows people who love one another deeply to be aware of the other person in the midst of all sorts of outward activity. Surely they understood something of what the other was experiencing in any given situation—such as the situation Mary encountered when visiting the place where Jesus was preaching, preoccupied with his work.

So, without saying so to the crowd lest they lose sight of the point he was making about their own obedience to God, when Jesus spoke of his true family, no doubt he was paying silent tribute to the woman outside—and no doubt she understood it.

Perhaps our embarrassed scramble to cover up Jesus' rudeness to his mother amuses them both. I hope so!

Way Will Open

lank walls bother us. Create a nice, clean, blank wall on a city street, and soon you will have graffiti or a mural. Blank walls in our homes are quickly adorned with pictures and other decorations. *Not just a blank wall*, the human spirit seems to cry! A canvas, maybe, which invites us into the picture, or a slogan, perhaps, which invites us to hear a voice and answer, but not a blank wall!

It could be that there lurks in us all a hidden dread of that final blank wall to which we have given the name of death. Too high to climb, too thick to tunnel through, and far too definite to ignore forever as we run down the paths in the garden where we play "life," this final wall is a forbidding horizon.

There is a long history of blank walls in our religious background. In one story we hear often, the wall is made of water (Exod 12–14). We know the scene: There they are, the Israelites, camped on the seashore. No vacation this, but a flight for survival. One minute, they were slaves in Egypt, lamenting their fate, unaware that anyone was listening. The next minute, a man they hardly knew, a man born to a Hebrew couple but raised as Pharaoh's grandson, a fugitive murderer long gone from Pharaoh's court, had planted himself before Pharaoh, demanding their release. A battle of plagues was waged between this stranger, well-known to us as Moses, and Pharaoh's magic-makers. Moses and his brother claimed to be speaking for the God the Israelites had forgotten they knew; Pharaoh's henchmen claimed to be speaking for Pharaoh. It was an uneven contest. Almost as suddenly as it had begun, it ended, with Pharaoh, his dead son in his arms, screaming at Moses to get out and take his countrymen with him *now*. They didn't have much notice—time to collect some booty, time to grab the unleavened bread dough, time to gather their children and their flocks, and then they were out of there. But it took Pharaoh even less time to change his mind. Now, here they were, camped on the seashore, with the Egyptian army in hot pursuit behind them and the unrelenting water closed before them. All that stood between them and sure destruction was a mysterious dark cloud. And everyone knows that you can't count on clouds for long.

Into that impossible moment came the voice of God making an impossible promise: "Way will open." The phrase was coined millennia later by the Quakers, but the idea is as old as the words "Let there be" (Gen 1:3). And way did open. The wind blew, the waters parted, and Moses told the fugitive slaves to go. It was the story of the Passover all over again—one minute, hopelessness; the next minute, an exit sign flashing in the dark. That same plot would repeat again and again over the long history of humanity with God, until at last the exit sign took the unmistakable shape of a cross pointing to the place where a huge stone lay rolled back from the entrance of an empty tomb. At last, at last, the final wall was breached—and for good.

Not everyone noticed then, and not everyone notices now. Not everyone believes it. Not everyone is too keen on following Christ through the breach. You never know about walls. They might fall in on you as you pass through. One wonders if something like that went on among those early Hebrews when way opened. No doubt some of them shouted, "Way to go!" and almost ran over each other in their headlong flight through the walls of water. But maybe some of them sat down on a rock and said, "This is impossible. Seas

don't just open up like that. There has to be a rational explanation. Let's think this thing out." And maybe some said,
"Don't go in there! It's an optical illusion! It's a trick! You'll
drown!" And perhaps some said to their children, "You come
back here and put on your boots and raincoats. You'll catch
your death in that water." And quite likely some said, "No
way *I'm* gonna go in there. Who knows what might happen!
No way, I tell you, no way." Maybe some of them went back
to Egypt as slaves. The story doesn't say.

Now most of us would probably like to imagine that when
the waters part at God's command, we'll be the first to charge
ahead, faithful and fearless. Chances are, though, that we may
not even notice that way has opened. Reasons may vary. Sometimes we are too busy hurrying along our accustomed path,
eyes fixed on our feet, minds fixed on today's preoccupation,
spirits transfixed by a deadline. Sometimes we have lived in a
particular set of boxes so long that we can't imagine any alter-
natives. "Thinking outside the box" can feel like a threat, not
a virtue. An anonymous author wrote, "To one who is walled
in, everything is wall, even an open door." Willful blindness
to the new cannot afford to see that way has opened.

There are antidotes, of course. One, recommended by spiritual teachers such as St. Benedict, is the art of pausing for
prayer before we begin our next task or activity. There are
many good reasons for this pause, but the goal is always to
keep an eye out for God's surprises and a foot at the ready to
take a new road. Once we get accustomed to it, the prayer
pause that stops us in our tracks won't seem quite so much an
intrusion as an opportunity to take a better route. Despite the
wisdom of time-managers, the fact is that prayer won't inter-
fere with our efficiency. We'll still get our appointed tasks taken
care of, but we won't feel like we're drowning in them.

Another antidote, closely related to the pause for prayer, is the practice of spiritual vigilance. This vigilance is not a wariness that looks at the passageway through the sea with a jaundiced eye and sits on a rock waiting for an explanation, or dismisses a saving reality as a mere illusion to be resisted, or lets the pathway close while looking for a raincoat. In other words, spiritual vigilance is not a form of self-protection against Divine Providence, as inexplicable as that Providence may sometimes seem. On the contrary, it is an attitude of constant attentiveness to possibility. Vigilance assumes faith. It requires the prayer that seeks in God's Word "a lamp for my feet, / and a light for my path" (Ps 119:105). It depends on the sort of radical openness and even reckless abandon that characterizes those who took Jesus seriously when he called them away from family, fishing nets, and life as they had always known it (Mark 1:16-20).

It's not every day that we find ourselves on the brink of the sea, with the Egyptians behind us and the waves before us, with nothing to hide us but a cloud. And yet it is probably more often than we realize. Sometimes the cause is dramatic: a lost job, a family breakup, a fire, a theft, an accident. Sometimes it's simply the awareness that we have reached what looks like a dead-end in our personal or spiritual lives.

The next time a blank wall looms before us, let's remember what our ancestors discovered on their flight from slavery: "Way will open!" And the way is not a nameless, faceless door. The way is a person: Jesus. From across the breach he calls to us, "I am the way! Come, follow me!" (see John 14:6; Matt 19:21).

The Folly of Solomon

Solomon grieves me.

You know the story. In response to his sacrifice of a thousand burnt offerings, God promises to give Solomon whatever he asks for (1 Kgs 3:4-5). Apparently, this generous Providence is expecting the usual wish list from a young man seated on the throne of his father's achievements and already well into the process of making important political alliances. The predictable list includes long life, wealth, and victory over enemies (1 Kgs 3:11). But Solomon surprises even God (who has seen everything and knows a thing or two about human foibles) when he makes this request instead: "I am a mere youth, not knowing at all how to act—I, your servant, among the people you have chosen, a people so vast that it cannot be numbered or counted. Give your servant, therefore, a listening heart to judge your people and to distinguish between good and evil" (1 Kgs 3:7-9).

As it turns out, young though he is, Solomon seems to know what the pearl of great price is, and he knows where to get it. Unlike the merchant in the Gospel story, he doesn't have to sell anything (Matt 13:45-46). He doesn't even have to dig for this treasure (Matt 13:44). All he has to do is ask the God of his father David, the One who has set him on his father's throne in turn. Solomon is clearly already wise. He knows his own limitations, he sees what his people need most, and he makes their good the one thing he asks for. God is pleased and gives him the whole package: both what he has asked for and what he hasn't. "I now do as you request," God says. "I give you a heart so wise and discerning that there has never been anyone like you until now, nor after you will there be anyone to equal you. In addition, I give you what you have not asked for: I give you such riches and glory that among kings there will be no one like you all your days" (1 Kgs 3:12-13). God then includes an important rider: "And *if you walk in my ways, keeping my statutes and commandments, as David your father did*, I will give you a long life" (1 Kgs 3:14; emphasis added). But Solomon has apparently already stopped listening. He has all those gifts to think about.

Solomon's first act after receiving the gift of discernment that he has requested is to demonstrate his newfound wisdom in the famous episode of the two mothers who come to him to resolve a tricky situation. These women had given birth at the same time, but one of their children died while the other survived. Now both women are claiming to have mothered the living child. In fact, they get into a hot argument over it right there in front of the king, who puts a stop to it by calling for a sword. When the sword comes, Solomon tells the servant who has brought it to cut the baby in two and give each woman half. One of the women says, "OK, the child won't be hers or mine. Go ahead and cut it in two!" (Good grief!) But the other one pleads, "No, please don't do that. Give her the baby." Looking to this woman, Solomon immediately says, "Let the baby live. Give it to this woman. She's the mother." The whole kingdom is in awe, recognizing that God has given Solomon the wisdom to judge aright. And his fame spreads. People come from all over to ask for his judgement. Even the Queen of Sheba "came from the ends of the earth to hear the wisdom of Solomon" (Matt 12:42; see 1 Kgs 10:1-10).

It doesn't hurt Solomon's reputation that after solidifying his vast kingdom according to God's promise, he sets about carrying out his father David's dream of building a great Temple to house God's presence in Jerusalem. David had in fact stockpiled all sorts of valuable materials for the project that God did not permit him to complete. But Solomon, as bidden, does. Seven years later, the result is magnificent (1 Kgs 5:15–6:38). God's glory fills the Temple as it filled the old portable Tent of Meeting that led Israel through the desert in the distant past (1 Kgs 8:10-11). And God appears once more to Solomon, as he had years before, saying, "I have heard the prayer of petition which you offered in my presence. I have consecrated this house which you have built and I set my name there forever; my eyes and my heart shall be there always" (1 Kgs 9:3). But once again, God adds the proviso: "As for you, *if you walk before me as David your father did, wholeheartedly and uprightly, doing all that I have commanded you, keeping my statutes and ordinances,* I will establish your royal throne over Israel forever, as I promised David your father" (1 Kgs 9:4-5; emphasis added). And once again, Solomon appears not to have listened.

Sadly, it seems that the only person in the world who did not consult the wisdom of Solomon was Solomon. Instead of heeding God's very specific condition, made with increasing urgency, the great king, master of all he surveyed, solidified his sovereignty among other peoples by making political marriages on all sides and taking well-placed concubines, although God's statutes and ordinances and pleas to the Israelites had forbidden them to marry those who worshipped other gods. God knew what would happen if they did. And, in Solomon's case, it happened. The author of 1 Kings claims that Solomon "held them close in love"—all seven hundred wives and three hundred concubines (1 Kgs 11:2-3)! In fact, he loved them so much that he built places of worship for all their pagan gods. The older he got, the more he honored them, and the more he turned away from his own God who had so richly blessed him. Solomon clearly forgot the proviso, but God did not. God expressed his displeasure to this king of wandering allegiance, telling him that the kingdom would be broken in two and most of it taken from his house. But, for the sake of God's beloved David, the heaviest consequences of Solomon's infidelity would be visited not on him, but on his son. And so it was (1 Kgs 11).

Solomon held the pearl of great price in his hand. It had been given to him without cost and without effort on his own part. But he threw it away. The pearl wasn't his great wealth or his political power or his status as the builder of the great Temple. It wasn't even his extraordinary ability to make good judgements, at least for people other than himself. The pearl was wisdom, in its most essential form. True wisdom is a deep communion with the God from whom all wisdom comes. That's what Solomon threw away so lightly.

Most of us will never be as wise as Solomon, but we can certainly be as foolish. The antidote? When God speaks, do what Solomon did not: listen!

Us and Them

Something there is that doesn't love a wall . . .

—*Robert Frost, "Mending Wall"*

When Jesus returned to his hometown of Nazareth, he brought his townspeople a powerful message of hope. In the synagogue, he read a passage from the prophet Isaiah that spoke to much of the misery people were enduring under Roman rule as well as under the ordinary tribulations of daily life everywhere:

> "The Spirit of the Lord is upon me,
>   because he has anointed me
>   to bring glad tidings to the poor.
> He has sent me to proclaim liberty to captives
>   and recovery of sight to the blind,
>   to let the oppressed go free,
> and to proclaim a year acceptable to the Lord." (Luke 4:18-19;
>   see Isa 61:1-2)

The key word "anointed" identified the one speaking as the promised messiah. To their astonishment, Jesus claimed this prophetic commission as his own: "Today this scripture passage is fulfilled in your hearing" (Luke 4:21). At first they welcomed the message with amazement and praise. But then doubt crept in. They had known Jesus for years. They had watched him grow up. But they had never noticed anything out of the ordinary about him or his family. How could he suddenly claim to be the messiah, with no previous hint?

Jesus obviously knew the Nazarenes better than they knew him. He could no doubt read in their familiar faces the questions that were brewing. He then threw fuel on the budding fire by identifying himself as a prophet in the tradition of Elijah and Elisha. He dared to compare his listeners unfavorably to two Gentiles, the widow of Zarephath who hosted Elijah (1 Kgs 17:9-24; Luke 4:25-26) and the Syrian leper Naaman healed by Elisha (2 Kgs 5:1-27; Luke 4:27). According to Jesus, these Gentiles had given Elijah and Elisha the acceptance that the people of Nazareth were beginning to refuse to one of their own. The villagers of Nazareth belonged to God's chosen people, the "us" among whom Jesus had grown up. The widow and the leper belonged to those outsiders to whom even the least of the chosen people were superior. The villagers were furious. Jesus had set Gentile outsiders above his own people. They rose up in a body to drive him out of town and throw him over the nearest cliff (Luke 4:29).

This was the first but far from the last time that Jesus undermined the rules that separated "us" from "them" in his day. As his critics complained, he ate with "sinners and tax collectors" (Mark 2:16-17), whose company he must have enjoyed since he sought it so readily. He even called a tax collector to become a disciple (Mark 2:14) and invited himself to eat in the house of another (Luke 19:5). But he also ate with the Pharisees who criticized him for eating with such inappropriate company. It was at table in a Pharisee's house that he refused to drive off a woman known to be a sinner when she intruded on the dinner party and washed his feet. In fact, he defended her to the host (Luke 7:44-47). He dared to touch proscribed lepers as he healed them even though they in fact posed an appalling danger to his own health (Mark 1:41), and he willingly broke the

law by touching them. He allowed a woman made ritually im-
pure by the affliction of longtime hemorrhages to catch on to
his cloak, and he healed her, thus reintegrating her back into
the community (Mark 5:25-34). He jousted verbally with two
quick-witted non-Israelite women, one a Canaanite and one a
Samaritan, apparently taking pleasure in the exchanges (Matt
15:21-28; John 4:4-27). And he promised the criminal crucified
next to him, another man outside the law, entry into paradise
(Luke 23:39-43). However he also made disciples of the wealthy
Joseph of Arimathea ("a distinguished member of the council";
Mark 15:43), and the Pharisee Nicodemus ("a ruler of the Jews";
John 3:1-15). After his death and resurrection he appeared to
the Pharisee Saul of Tarsus, notorious persecutor of the young
Church, to send him to preach the gospel to the very Gentiles
his own neighbors would have rejected (Acts 9:1-16). For Jesus,
no one—male or female, rich or poor, law-abiding or law-
breaker, Jew or Gentile—was ever beyond the pale.

Jesus went even farther. He went after the religious leaders,
not to condemn them as we often imagine, but to persuade
them to throw their lot in with the growing reign of God from
which no one is excluded except by choice. We see him besting
them in arguments; we see him frustrated and angry with
them; we see him accusing them of hypocrisy. But we also see
him grieving over the hardness of heart that kept them locked
up in their own small, exclusive world of superiority, inacces-
sible even to the God they claimed to serve. So persistently
are they presented as Jesus' enemies that we sometimes tend
to overlook the fact that they were therefore included in his
commandment to love even one's enemies and to pray for
them (Matt 5:44)—and he did both (Luke 23:34). Being, as St.
Paul called him, God's own love in human flesh (Rom 8:39),
he could do no other. Conversion, not destruction, was his
desire for them.

There is a provocative line verse in Psalm 57: "They dug a pit in my path, / but fell in it themselves" (v. 7). It describes Jesus' enemies well. We may find ourselves cheering the downfall of the hostile and dangerous, but Jesus didn't. In a very real sense, through his death on the cross, he followed all his enemies into the pit of death where they had fallen so he could retrieve them and bring them home where they belonged—unless they absolutely refused to come. *That* outcome, that homecoming, he would expect us to cheer.

The letter to the Ephesians paints a powerful picture of Jesus breaking down once and for all the barrier that divides *us* from *them*: "But now in Christ Jesus you who once were far off have become near by the blood of Christ. For he is our peace, he who made both one and broke down the dividing wall of enmity, through his flesh, . . . that he might create in himself one new person in place of the two, thus establishing peace, and might reconcile both with God, in one body, through the cross" (Eph 2:13-16). The villagers in Nazareth might have been dismayed to discover that these lines refer to their own cherished "dividing wall of enmity" between the chosen people to which they belonged and the Gentile "outsiders." But we also must face the fact that these verses refer to every *us* and *them* between whom we ourselves have drawn uncrossable boundaries: *we* the virtuous, *they* the sinners; *we* the successful, *they* life's failures; *we* the right color, the right nationality, the right social or economic class, *they* everyone else.

Robert Frost had it almost right, but not quite. *Someone* there is who doesn't love a wall . . .

Here I Am . . . But Who Are You?

The boy Samuel was still a resident apprentice with the old priest Eli when he was rudely awakened by an unrecognized voice one night as he slept in the sanctuary at Shiloh (predecessor to the Jerusalem Temple of later centuries). Eli was the only other person around, it seems, so Samuel quite naturally got up from his sleeping mat, perhaps grumbling a little, as one does when awakened in the middle of the night, and ran in to ask Eli what he wanted. But Eli hadn't called. When the same thing happened two more times, Eli understood what was happening and told the boy that if the voice woke him again, he should say, "Speak, LORD, for your servant is listening" (1 Sam 3:9).

Samuel seems to have been an obedient boy, but he didn't quite answer as Eli had told him to. Instead of saying, "Speak, Lord," he said rather less politely and precisely, "Speak, for your servant is listening" (3:10).

This passage is often used at retreats, workshops, and talks about finding one's personal calling. When you feel a sense of call, a lecturer will say, you might ignore it at first, but if it keeps returning, turn to God in prayer to find out what God is calling you to do.

Good advice, but it is worth noting that the biblical passage is also something of a cautionary tale. When we feel an inner urge or call, perhaps we should be warned by Samuel's small disobedience. To turn to God and say, "Speak, Lord, your servant is listening," is one thing. To respond instead, as if to the empty air, "Speak, your servant is listening," is exactly what we often do when we feel an inner urge but don't take the time or trouble to identify who or what it is that is calling us. We feel the tug and obey it, as if, like Samuel, we were asleep when it came and haven't quite awakened enough to pay real attention to what's going on.

What if, without realizing it, we stumble too quickly from urge to action, only to discover that the voice belonged to the tempting picture of chocolate cake in the refrigerator or the kind of curiosity that has a lethal effect on cats or the spontaneous chemistry that flames up when we meet someone who attracts us physically? Prompt obedience to God's voice is a good thing, but prompt obedience to unidentified voices can get us into a lot of trouble.

There are lots of voices buzzing in our mind's ears every day. When one seems louder and stronger than usual, and we feel the urge to hop off our sleeping mat and go and do as it says, we might be better off taking the time to stop and say what Samuel didn't: "Here I am, but who are you?"

Voice and Word

When John the Baptist made his dramatic appearance in the Judean desert, John's Gospel reports that the religious leaders turned out in force to find out who he was. They tried traditional labels and expectations: "Are you the Messiah? No? Then are you Elijah? Not Elijah either? Then the Prophet? Not him either? Then who are you? We have to report back" (see John 1:19-22). They were anxious to fit this odd character—clearly somehow prophetic—into a familiar box so they would know how to deal with him. They should have known better. God and God's messengers have an irritating habit of breaking out of boxes.

But we are often guilty of the same management strategy. The unfamiliar makes us nervous. We would like to assign the proper box or label to God-with-us so that we can call on a pre-planned response. Shepherd? We'll turn ourselves into biddable sheep, perhaps with a good deal of interior grumbling that we hope the Shepherd will not overhear. Teacher? We'll sit down at imaginary desks and try to look attentive, maybe whipping out our notebooks so we can take assiduous notes. But St. Augustine, commenting on John's Gospel in the fourth century, offered a far more dangerous set of labels: "The voice is John," he wrote, but "Christ is the Word." The only appropriate response to voice and Word is to listen.

Real listening, though, makes us uncomfortably vulnerable. The kind of listening that joins the words we hear with pre-planned answers helps us maintain control. But *The Rule of*

St. Benedict recommends a different kind of listening. Benedict counsels all believers, not only those who live by his guidance, to listen "with the ear of your heart" (Prologue 1). This kind of listening, however, opens us up to allow the Word to say what he will and go where he will, even into the very depths of our hearts, a place we often keep safely walled up and protected.

The Word makes demands that we commit ourselves to meet when we allow ourselves to be serious listeners. St. Benedict's admonition to listen means a very intense listening that responds with obedience. And the obedient heart acts. It puts into practice what it has heard. In other words, it surrenders the self-protection we so cherish. St. Benedict calls that particular form of armor our "own will." This isn't the free will that is God's gift to us. Rather, it is the parody of free will that we seem to prefer when we equate freedom with the right to do anything we want, with no reference to God or neighbor or even our own inmost truth. Listening with the ear of the heart requires that we choose—freely and responsibly, with a lot of help from God—to ignore that small voice inside of us that says things like, "What's in it for me?" Or, "Hey, I've gotta take care of Number One—me!" The will that is truly free of all the constraints with which we tend to bind ourselves can choose to act on what the Word has said. And that Word is always first and foremost Christ who loves us.

Human beings are survivors at heart, and rightly so. We were created to live fully and finally in the new creation wrought by Christ—that is, to live forever beyond the doors of death in a place we cannot yet see. But as very determined survivors, often blinded by our too-small understanding of what survival means, we tend to dislike vulnerability. It threatens our safety, or so it seems. However, as Michael Casey, OCSO, points out in his book *The Road to Eternal Life*, becoming vulnerable to God speaking to us is absolutely essential to the process of growing into the person we are created to be—

the person who will not only survive beyond death but will find the reign of God in its fullness to be a perfect fit.

Listening to the voice that speaks to us through Scripture and the Rule and the vicissitudes of everyday life is our project as human beings so beloved by God that God's personal Word was born among us to lead the way to that final home in God's reign. Today is a good day to hone our listening skills, with God's ever-present help and one another's support and encouragement. Together we will listen with the ears of our hearts—vulnerable, unencumbered, and completely free—as we travel the road to eternal life.

Surely Not I, Lord?

Throughout the Church year, we stop from time to time to remember the men and women who have lived out literally Christ's exhortation to lay down our lives for one another out of love (John 15:13).

When we aspire to such love, let us remember one such believer from the past so we may hear his questions to us in the present. St. Ignatius of Antioch, a Syrian bishop, was martyred in Rome around AD 107. On the journey from his home in Syria to his death, Ignatius wrote seven letters to various churches. He wrote on a number of subjects, but he spoke with especially vivid eloquence of his ardent desire for martyrdom. Certainly, in our own epoch of religious violence, many contemporary Christians from St. Ignatius's part of the world and elsewhere are suffering torture and death for their commitment to Christ and the gospel. But those of us who live less threatened lives might squirm a bit at the vehemence of Ignatius's plea to be allowed to die the death to which he has been condemned, without the intervention of well-meaning fellow Christians.

Nonetheless, Ignatius reminds us of the discomforting challenge of Jesus, who said there was no greater love than to lay down one's life for others. Jesus, of course, lived and died by that uncompromising love. And, lest we give pious thanks and go on about our business without being tempted to follow his example, he left us the commandment, "*As I have loved you,* so you also should love one another" (John 13:34; emphasis added).

Ignatius responded to that commandment according to his personal call at a time when Christians were actively persecuted. We are asked to respond to the same commandment according to our personal call in our own present circumstances, whatever they might be. For some, the response may very well be fidelity to Christ in the face of torture and death. But for many of us, it will simply be fidelity to Christ in the humdrum demands of everyday life. It will likely be a fidelity that requires not a single dramatic surrender but steady perseverance in ordinary things. If we are asked to lay down our lives minute by minute by spending the precious wealth of our time, our energy, our company, our attentiveness, our talents, or simply our willingness to be of service, the sacrifice may not be as spectacular as Ignatius's death in the arena, but it will be just as valuable. Washing dishes so someone else doesn't have to has none of the drama of being torn to bits by wild beasts—but it may demand just as much love.

Ignatius gave a unique twist to the laying down of his life. He understood his martyrdom not simply as a death died willingly in imitation of Christ. Rather he understood it as a death died willingly *for the same reason* that Christ died. He left us a graphic description of his purpose: "Let me be food for the wild beasts, for they are my way to God. I am God's wheat and shall be ground by their teeth so that I may become Christ's pure bread" (Letter to the Romans). The allusion is, of course, to the Eucharist. Ignatius laid down his life not to copy Christ, but—in Christ and with Christ—to feed the life of Christ's Body with his own.

Ignatius's words raise two questions that we must ask ourselves: When I lay down my life for others, whom am I feeding? And whom am I seeking to build up? Whatever offering we make of our time, energy, company, attentiveness, and service, we make that offering not simply to do what Jesus would do, but, in obedience to Christ, to feed Christ's Body with his own love visibly embodied in ours. Anything less is apt to feed and build up only our own ego—a ravenous beast, to be sure, and perfectly capable of grinding us down to fine flour for bread—but not to build up the Body of Christ in love.

Arrest, torment, and death were the price Ignatius paid for his fidelity to Christ. Although we expect to pay a lesser price, we ought not to imagine that our own fidelity to Christ's command to love as he did will always be rewarded with gratitude, blessing, or praise. There is a telling line in Psalm 38: "They . . . attack me for seeking what is good" (v. 21). "They" may be the resentful, the jealous, those who fail to understand—or they may be our own doubts, hesitations, or failures of nerve in the face of hostility. And these may be just as frightening to face as the wild animals in the arena.

Lay down my life? Surely not I, Lord? St. Ignatius, pray for us!

A Different Desert

A leper came to him [and kneeling down] begged him and said, "If you wish, you can make me clean." Moved with pity, he stretched out his hand, touched him, and said to him, "I do will it. Be made clean." The leprosy left him immediately, and he was made clean.

—*Mark 1:40-42*

The desert of his temptation was not the last desert Jesus met. Shortly into the public ministry to which he had committed himself in defiance of the Tempter, Jesus found himself faced with a leper pleading for healing. Here was a wasteland created not by sun and sand but by hideous disease. Here was a man who had once lived a normal life. Perhaps he had a wife and children. Perhaps he was respected by his neighbors. Perhaps he had grown wheat to supply the village with bread. Perhaps he had cultivated olive trees to supply oil to soothe sunbaked skin, or to give lamplight on a dark night, or to season a simple diet of barley bread. Leprosy had cut off every "perhaps" that might have defined his life.

Like the desert of rock and sand and scrub through which Jesus had passed into the busy streets and marketplaces of Galilee, this man's life had become empty, sterile, purposeless. He had lost family, work, community—even his name. The evangelist calls him simply "a leper"—a face, a marred body, a threat to those around him, but no longer Joshua or Simeon or Judah, cherished son, spouse, friend. Just "a leper." He could exchange kind words, a loving touch, simple companionship with no one now, because he had become a danger to everyone. He could feed no one, except perhaps fellow lepers with whom he might have shared the bread that family members sometimes left for the leper colony. He could produce nothing for anyone. He could do nothing but survive—and that not for long.

But the Word, now made flesh as Jesus of Nazareth, had known the primal chaos, the *tohu wa-bohu* in Hebrew, that the Scriptures say existed before the world was made (Gen 1:2). Translator and commentator Robert Alter says the phrase means "emptiness" or "futility" and is sometimes associated with "the trackless vacancy of the desert." At God's command, the Word had, as it were, dived beneath the dark surface of this primal chaos, pictured in Genesis 1 as a dark sea. The Word had traveled among the nameless, purposeless, isolated possibilities it contained and had drawn them forth to become sun, moon, stars, fig trees, whales, eagles, and all that we call "creation." Finally came human beings, the crown of the work the Word had done (Gen 1:1-31).

At Jesus' baptism, just a few verses before this meeting with the leper, he emerged from the Jordan waters. The presence of dove and Voice identified him as the beginning of the *new creation*, the Word made flesh who would restore and transform the ruins wrought by the first human beings into full, fresh life (Mark 1:10-11).

So Jesus looks at the wasted, barren, ruined body before him and sees the human being buried there, beneath the emptiness and futility of the trackless vacancy of a life turned into a desert. And he draws that human being forth—draws the man, the son, the brother, the spouse, the father, the neighbor—draws him out to take his place in the ordinary world from which he had been banished. At the sound of Jesus' voice and the touch of his hand, the prophetic promise is realized: "The wilderness and the parched land will exult; / the [desert] will rejoice and bloom" (Isa 35:1). The leper is made clean.

That leper is long gone now, but Jesus Christ, crucified and risen, continues to make of us all a new creation that will flourish long after the old one has disappeared. Again and again, he says to us in our sinfulness, our failures, our broken families and communities, our lost purposes and our lost hopes, what he said to the leper: "Come out of that desert. Live!"

Suffer Many Tribulations?

"We must suffer many tribulations and thus enter the kingdom of God."

—Acts 14:22 (*translation of the Benedictine Abbey of St. Walburga*)

This little bit of cheerful news greets our Abbey community first thing in the morning every other Tuesday. It is the verse selected to introduce Psalm 6, the first psalm of Matins (early morning prayer), and the first of the seven "penitential psalms." Since going back to bed and pulling the covers over our heads is not an option, we have to wrestle with the God it seems to suggest. Is this a God who charges a grisly admission fee to the kingdom Jesus proclaimed as good news? A God all too ready to punish us for the sins for which we beg forgiveness in the penitential psalms? A God who calls for fear and dread?

Quite the contrary. Have you ever found yourself at a social gathering where you just didn't fit in? Everyone else was measuring success by goals you didn't share. People around you were pursuing relationships that made you uncomfortable, praising successes you couldn't understand, lamenting failures that looked to you like success. You felt like a stranger among strangers and just wanted to go home.

Consider the kingdom of God in this light. It is not a geographical place but the way of life proclaimed and lived by Jesus himself in all he said and did. It is governed by two laws only: "You shall love the Lord, your God, with all your heart, with all your soul, and with all your mind" (Matt 22:37) and "You shall love your neighbor as yourself" (Matt 22:39). Jesus later amended the second commandment: "I give you a new commandment: love one another. As I have loved you, so you also should love one another" (John 13:34). Context clarifies what he meant: he gave this commandment at the Last Supper, on the vigil of his passion and death. Jesus devotes endless stories and exhortations to descriptions of life and relationships defined by these laws as he tries to help us understand the kingdom of God as God's goal for us.

But what if we were to cross death's threshold and find ourselves embraced by the fullness of God's reign, only to discover that we did not and could not fit in? What ultimate misery! The God who loves us would never want us to endure it. So we have to get ready here to belong there. That's one way of looking at the Christian's life work of conversion. And it's sometimes very tough, as we have all learned. That's where the "tribulations" come in.

This verse is not a threat of some kind but a description of reality. Most of us don't yet fit completely into the life of the kingdom of God for which we long, but we have a lifetime to get ready. It's sometimes a struggle, sometimes painful, sometimes more suffering than joy. This arduous process is not some kind of punishment but a gift from the God who loves us enough to have joined us by taking on our humanity in Jesus Christ—he who lived, suffered, died, and rose from the dead so that we could live into the promised kingdom for always.

Honey from the Rock

All suffering entails loss: loss of a loved one, a friend, a home, work we loved, a way of life we had embraced, the future we had planned, the capacity to move about freely, to laugh, to play. Loss leaves us feeling robbed. It casts us as victims of someone else's violence. At times, when we are unable to identify any other cause for our loss, we may even consider ourselves victims of *God's* violence.

We are not mere victims, though, no matter what we lose. We may not have chosen to suffer, but we can choose how we cope. Not immediately, perhaps. Not till we've caught our breath, licked our wounds, wept out our hurt, and raged at our fate. But eventually, we can and must and do make choices. Suffering can enlarge us or diminish us. Choosing how to deal with it is key.

First we must face the empty spaces left by our loss. In the beginning we may run from them, pretend they aren't there, fill them up with frenetic activity, cram them with new furniture, stuff them with food and drink, do *anything* to put off the dreaded moment when we have to go in, sit down, and listen to the sound of emptiness bouncing off the walls. Like mountain caves carved by time, water, and wind, these hollow places offer their own kind of peace. It isn't true that time heals all wounds, but it is true that time at least stops the worst of the bleeding. Tears contribute to the healing. A healthy human outlet, they can soften the sharp edges that re-open the hurt, put out the angry fire that loss kindles, wash away the confusion that clouds memories we want to cherish, and leave our empty places fresh and clean.

But first we have to go there. Often we have to take the trip in stages: five minutes, twenty, half an hour, until we lose the fear that the emptiness will destroy us. In fact, inhabiting our hollows makes room for us to grow, to make friends with ourselves in a new way, to discover God in unexpected places. If you've ever climbed up to a high cave and sat there looking out over the landscape below, you know what surprises new perspectives can bring to places we thought we knew.

Inhabiting our hollows does not mean walling ourselves into them. Blocking up the entrance (and exit) so we can feast alone in gloom on a diet of bitter herbs and gall won't give us relief. Gnawing on memories and regrets until they start to rot won't give us the solace of solitude. Caves so occupied offer a standing invitation to predators. A resident mountain lion or snake will scare away visitors, leaving us lonely. Then the predators are more likely than not to turn on us. Self-preoccupation, self-pity, resentment, jealousy of those who seem untouched by pain and loss, and abandonment of moral disciplines are hungry beasts that swallow up the human spirit. It's not for nothing that 1 Peter 5:8 warns: "Be sober and vigilant. Your opponent the devil is prowling around like a roaring lion looking for [someone] to devour."

If, instead of closing ourselves into our grief, we sit in our newly-hollowed caves and look out, we may find that the great wind which is God's Spirit will blow through the emptiness, carrying away all the remnants of our morbid feasts. We can let them go. Then we will find that instead of predators, God will send honeybees. Some species of bees build their hives in the dark safety of a cave. The bees in our caves will set about their work, busily gathering all the flavors of the world around us and within us, a world seen afresh from the perspective of our pain. They will transmute what they have gathered into wild honey. Soon friends, neighbors, and strangers will climb the path to our empty places not to bring us comfort but to find it. The wisdom distilled from our suffering by the busy work of the bees will strengthen them to deal with their own burdens. The compassion that has grown in the hollows left by our loss will sustain them. The love that has deepened and matured through our decision to refuse entry to the lion and the snake will feed our visitors in ways they themselves did not expect and may not understand.

That's the thing about the gospel. Jesus gives us only two commandments: "You shall love the Lord, your God, with all your heart, with all your being, with all your strength, and with all your mind, and your neighbor as yourself" (Luke 10:27). Nowhere is it written: "Except, of course, when you are suffering." When, through the alchemy of God's grace working through our own choices, we find our most bitter suffering turned into honey to feed the multitudes, we are freed from one of the worst of our losses: the loss of a sense of purpose.

Suffering in itself seems so meaningless. Suffering transformed into love fulfills the central purpose of human life as God intends it. We have only to look at Jesus on the cross to see it. Indeed we have all benefitted from that suffering, and that time spent in the hollowed-out cave of Jesus, that rock-hewn tomb (Luke 23:53).

It was promised, you know, this transformation:

"O that my people would heed me,
that [they] would walk in my ways!
At once I would . . .
satisfy [them] with honey from the rock." (Ps 81:14, 17)

Prayers and Psalms

Seat of Wisdom

Mary, seat of wisdom, pray for us.

—*The Litany of Loreto*

Near the back of Saint John's Abbey Church in Collegeville, Minnesota, a small Marian chapel houses a twelfth-century wood carving of Mother and Child known as the "Throne of Wisdom." Mary sits on a chair. On her knees, the Child, a miniature adult rather than a baby, sits with right hand upraised in blessing and left hand clasped around a book. Both figures are regally dressed and wear expressions of profound serenity. One has the impression that in their stillness, everything has been known, everything said, everything accepted.

Mary as the *sedes sapientiae* (a Latin title translated either as "throne of wisdom" or "seat of wisdom") appeared often in medieval iconography at a time when Christian imagery frequently drew inspiration from court life. Mary as the seat of wisdom is a majestic figure enthroning the Christ, who was called by St. Paul "the power of God and the wisdom of God" (1 Cor 1:24). She is often seated on a throne herself. Her child is the adult Christ who has triumphed over sin and death by dying on the cross and rising victorious. The statue at St. John's, like many others, is a victory hymn in wood.

As a statue, a painting, or a title for Mary in the Litany of Loreto, the "seat of wisdom" offers comfort, hope, and strength at times when the defeated forces of sin and death seem to rise up again to threaten our peace. But at such times, I find that

I do not turn to the image of Mother and Son enthroned in majesty but to a different image of the seat of wisdom: the image of the Mother seated beneath the cross, her dead Son in her lap, an image commonly known as the *pietà*.

Michelangelo's *Pietà*, carved in marble and displayed in St. Peter's Basilica in Rome, is perhaps the best known and most beloved of many *pietà*s. Here too serenity prevails, but it is the serenity not of triumphant majesty but of humanity experienced to its darkest depths and then accepted with the patient perseverance of love. The Son, tortured and murdered by the worst distortion evil could wreak through human beings, has descended not only into death but into the murky place of wordless half-life beyond, a place called "hell" in our Creed. He bears the scars still, but he is undefeated and undestroyed. He seems to be sleeping after his ordeal, but we know that from that marble stillness he will return for us, as he promised.

The *Pietà* assures us that we will never be alone even in our grimmest moments. The Mother has understood, supported, and accompanied her Son into the depths, not physically but spiritually. Her face wears the peace of one who has refused nothing, not even her Son's death and descent into hell. And like us, she cannot claim the protection of divinity we sometimes imagine he hid behind (though Philippians 2:5-11 assures us that he did not). Indeed he refused nothing of the human condition, except sin.

In biblical literature, wisdom teaches us how to live fully but faithfully within the realities of mortal life. So when the waters of chaos rise around me and the dark waters of self-interest—mine or someone else's—threaten to pull me down into lightless shadows, it is to this *Pietà* that I turn and cry, "Seat of Wisdom, pray for us!"

Psalm 63:
Prayer Before the Blessed Sacrament

O God, you are my God . . .
for you my soul is thirsting.
For you my flesh is pining,
like a dry, weary land without water.
I have come before you in the holy place,
to behold your strength and your glory. . . .
My soul shall be filled as with a banquet.

—Psalm 63:2-3, 6a

Hungry? Nothing in the pantry or fridge appeals? A drawerful of takeout menus offers no help? So often we imagine our hunger to be for the tangible—food, company, fun—when what we really desire is the intangible. The "More," as the late Karl Rahner used to call it. Our deepest hunger cries out for communion with God, a hunger built into us from the start.

The intangible becomes tangible in the Eucharist where Christ comes to us under the signs of food and drink. In our post-Vatican II world, we are accustomed to going straight to Eucharistic communion to satisfy our hunger. But prior to the Council, when circumstances deprived Catholics of ready access to the bread and cup for centuries, they discovered a solution in the form of Eucharistic devotions. Seeing the Eucharistic Christ in the Blessed Sacrament exposed gave them the access for which they hungered. Seeing in faith, they found, is a mode of being in communion.

Their ingenious wisdom perdures in the current revival of Eucharistic adoration. "I have come before you in the holy place to see your strength and your glory," we still pray in the psalmist's words. Wait! Strength? Presence, yes. Self-giving love, yes. Communion in that invisible realm we call the heart, yes. But strength?

Precisely. In the Eucharist, we receive the Paschal Christ, present in his dying and rising. Think of the strength that carried Jesus through it all. In his passion, enduring human behavior at its ugliest, he faced the most powerful temptation possible. We might imagine the voice of the Tempter sounding in his mind: "Don't let them do that! Go on, wipe them out in one fell and very satisfying swoop! That's how you deal with enemies, not by loving them!" In other words, trade in your deepest truth as God's love made flesh, and use the divine power to win a quick victory and spare yourself all that agony! But throughout Jesus' passion, as the temptation must surely have mounted with his pain and weakness, he refused. As Jesus died on the cross, he did not cry out, "Father, destroy all these cruel, heartless torturers." He prayed, "Father, forgive them, they know not what they do" (Luke 23:34). Loving one's enemies under circumstances like this takes unimaginable strength of will. That is the strength we see by faith in the Eucharistic Christ.

And to see is to become, as St. Paul says: "All of us, gazing . . . on the glory of the Lord, are being transformed into the same image from glory to glory" (2 Cor 3:18). St. John adds that we "shall be like him, for we shall see him as he is" (1 John 3:2). In the Eucharist, we see Christ as he is for us now: the Bread of Life wrought by Love who never gave up loving, however great the provocation. Hunger of every kind weakens us, sometimes to death. But here we see Love strong enough to feed what the forces of sin and death had attempted to starve:

the image of the God of love embedded in the depths of our being. Truly in our seeing we are "filled as with a banquet."

And, seeing, we become what we see: in Christ, God's bread for a hungry world.

Holy Door

In the name of the Father, and of the Son, and of the Holy Spirit.

—*Sign of the Cross*

E very twenty-five years, or sometimes more often, the Church celebrates a jubilee year. It begins with the solemn opening of the Holy Door at St. Peter's Basilica in Rome. But we have no need to wait so long or go so far. We have the holiest of doors always at our fingertips—literally. Whenever we sign ourselves with the cross of Christ—in the name of the Father, Son, and Holy Spirit—we open that door and enter into God's presence. Perhaps more accurately, we cross the threshold into awareness of the God who is always with us but often unnoticed.

What do we find there? Looking to the Eucharist as teacher of prayer, we learn to expect a place of communion. From the opening greeting at Mass—"The Lord be with you"—"with" becomes the hallmark of a path into deeper and deeper togetherness with one another in Christ. We note first our own common identity as sinners seeking and finding God's mercy. Then we settle down for a conversation between the God who creates with words and us who are created as hearers, made in the image of a speaking God. God's Word meets us everywhere in the liturgy, and everywhere we are invited to "talk back" in responses, acclamations, prayers, and—above all—in the depths of a listening heart. This creative conversation culminates in sacramental communion beyond words with Christ in his Eucharistic Body and Blood and in the mystical Body gathered together in the mystery of his death and resurrection.

When it's all over, it isn't over. The presider sends us off with a final blessing given and received in the Sign of the Cross. But that sign does not mark the closing of the door we came in through; it marks our passage out into the broader holy place we call "the world." There, as the Eucharistic celebration has taught us, we must also seek or make places of communion marked by conversation.

Christ promised: "I am with you always" (Matt 28:20). Sometimes we may not seem to hear God's voice even with the ears of the heart (see *The Rule of St. Benedict*; Prologue 1), but we should not conclude that God is not there. Even when all we seem to hear is silence, we live in what might be called the ongoing conversation of being: God always speaking the creative Word, and creation responding by existing and growing soundlessly into that Word. Solitude—or worse, isolation—may sometimes be our experience, but it is never our fundamental reality. Life is not a monologue delivered in emptiness. It is always being and conversing "with"—with God and with one another and, in some sense, with all that is. We do this as the ultimate "we," the Body of Christ crucified and risen.

So let us make the Sign of the Cross reverently. It is the holy door that leads through death to the fullness of life we yearn for.

Confiteor: We Confess

I confess to almighty God
and to you, my brothers and sisters,
that I have greatly sinned,
in my thoughts and in my words,
in what I have done and in what I have failed to do,
through my fault, through my fault,
through my most grievous fault;
therefore I ask blessed Mary ever-Virgin,
all the Angels and Saints,
and you, my brothers and sisters,
to pray for me to the Lord our God.

—*The Roman Missal*

Since the Middle Ages, Catholic worshippers have offered this prayer in the Introductory Rites of the Eucharistic celebration. At one time, the words were said by an acolyte representing the people, who had no speaking part in the Mass. In our day, the assembly has appropriated the text as our own. This opening part of the Eucharistic celebration is often referred to as the "gathering" rite—a word that is deceptively innocuous. It might refer to the gathering of family for a Sunday meal, or the gathering of friends to share a glass of wine, or any sort of social get-together. But at Mass it refers to the hard work of taking a motley crowd of wildly different and even conflicting individual Christians and beginning the Eucharistic process of forging and re-forging us into the one Body of Christ bonded in love through the power of the cross.

Let's take a look at a typical parish's Sunday Mass. Friends and strangers, rivals and opponents hurry into church from wherever they have been—from traffic, from the parking lot competition for the perfect spot, from whatever arguments it took at home to get everyone ready to go. Ushers do their best to fit everyone in and keep the front pews filled. But when Mr. Cashmere Sport Coat spots young Ragged Cutoffs in his designated pew, he retreats to another row. Mr. and Mrs. Natural Fibers frown darkly at Ms. Fox Fur Stole as she makes space for them to squeeze past. Three matching Tank-Tops-Over-Tights glower at all adults on principle. Crisp and ironed Cotton-and-Denim want to sit in the back for a quick exit, but they veer away at the sight of God-Loves-Me-Whether-I-Do-Laundry-or-Not in the last pew.

Mass begins. At the appropriate moment, the presider intones, "I confess . . ." And that ancient text levels the playing field. Whatever else we might have been outside the church doors, here we admit that we are all—each and every one of us—sinners in search of forgiveness and reconciliation. Because for whatever reason, God's pardon matters to us. And we join each other in asking, because no matter what we're wearing, we're all in this sinful world together, headed for God's reign. Then we appeal to all the unseen members of this gathering, the ones who have gone on before us and hold open the door, because people in heaven really do care about the people still on earth—khakis, cutoffs, and all. Mary, the saints, and the angels are all involved in our lives, whoever we are, because they also belong to God's reign and await us there. For them, the commandment to love one's neighbor—and in that reign, everyone is neighbor—has a force and an intensity we can barely begin to imagine.

"Amen," we go on to say. There, now. We may look the same as we did when we came in. Our neighbors may be wearing the same clothes they had on when we sat down. And, to be honest, we may not have paid much attention to the words we said. But God did. So, at some level we do not see, impelled by the Holy Spirit drawing us forward, we have joined hands and set off together again on the road to the place where all are clothed in Christ and all divisions disappear (Gal 3:27-28).

Prayer for the Preparation of the Bread

Blessed are you, Lord God of all creation,
for through your goodness we have received
the bread we offer you:
fruit of the earth and work of human hands,
it will become the bread of life.

—*The Roman Missal*

One morning at Mass the fog of insufficient sleep parted long enough for me to hear "fruit of the earth and work of human hands." Where had the words come from? From a prayer I had never really paid much attention to before that moment.

As we blessed God for gathering together the materials to be made into the Eucharistic offering and putting them in our hands, it occurred to me that the prayer hinted at a grace before meals. I suddenly thought of Sister Augustina, who for years uncounted was the smiling provider of delicious loaves of homemade bread at every meal eaten by our monastic community and guests—to say nothing of hungry families in the neighborhood! As age began to slow Sister Augustina down, we tried to get her recipes for posterity, but there had been no cookbooks in the little Bavarian farm village where she had grown up between two world wars. Recipes were a matter of mind and fingers, passed on by word of mouth. So Sister Augustina obligingly taught her young apprentices while she worked: "Take some flour, a handful of yeast, a pinch or two of salt, some water—warm water, mind, not too hot"—and "Knead the dough till it feels ready." Fruits of the earth and work of human hands made ready for the table.

And so is the bread for the Eucharistic table made: from the fruit of the earth and the work of human hands. That is, with what has been given to us and what we have made of it. Flour ground by human labor, from the wheat cultivated by many hands, using tools created by human minds, and forged in factories employing many human skills. God made us collaborators in the work of creation in those long-ago beginnings remembered in the book of Genesis, and God still honors that arrangement. So we bless the God who put the fruit of the earth into human hands to be prepared for offering.

But bread and the wine that goes with it are not the only gifts to be offered. Old devotionals once urged us to put ourselves on the paten with the bread. They sound quaint now, but they spoke to the heart of the Eucharist: the gift of bread will become the Body of Christ, but by communion in the holy Bread, so will we. And the lives we bring to the table to be so transformed are, like the gift of bread, the product of what we have been given and what we have made of it. But not alone. *We* are the fruit of our world's history and the work of many human hands—the hands that delivered us from our mother's womb, the hands that washed away the tears provoked by skinned knees, the hands that packed lunches for us, the hands that wrote vocabulary words and mathematical equations on the board for us, the hands that helped us up when we fell, the hands that received applications for work or school, the hands that built the homes we live in and the places where we work, the hands that held ours as we stood before God to vow our lives either as spouses or as consecrated religious. So many hands!

And Sister Augustina's were among them—encouraging, cleaning up, and mending lives with a kind smile and a wise word, making them ready to become God's bread for the world, as she herself was.

Blessed are you, Lord God of all creation, for through your goodness we have received the lives we offer you, fruit of the earth's story and work of human hands. May we become in Christ the bread of life!

The Eucharistic Doxology: A Prepositional Spirituality

Through him, and with him, and in him,
O God, almighty Father,
in the unity of the Holy Spirit,
all glory and honor is yours,
for ever and ever.
Amen.

—*The Roman Missal*

"Concentrate on the verbs," my English teacher told us. "They're the most important words."

"Pay attention to the nouns," said another teacher.

But no one ever mentioned the prepositions—small, uninteresting bits of language—necessary but apparently needing no attention. "Function words," the dictionary calls them.

But they are much more than that. Prepositions are bridges that connect people, places, and times. They reveal relationships. Not too long ago, a priest friend quoted a wise old seminary professor who said, "It's all in the prepositions." In the doxology concluding the Eucharistic prayer, the prepositions lay out for us not only the theological bones of the Eucharistic offering but also the very framework of the life we are called to live.

There is an eighth-century Latin phrase you may have heard: *lex orandi, lex credendi.* It means, "The law of prayer is the law of belief." The principle is modern enough: repeat anything often enough and people will believe it—an idea happily exploited today by the advertising world. In other words, what we say and sing together over and over in prayer, liturgical or personal, forms what we believe. The Latin phrase actually describes a two-way street: prayer shapes our belief, and belief shapes our prayer. Thus the very language of the liturgy becomes a tool for our ongoing spiritual growth and conversion because beliefs ground the way we live.

The Eucharist holds primacy of place in that work of conversion, inviting us into the fullness of Christ's death and resurrection so that we can gradually grow out of the death-grip of self-centered sin and into the freedom of the life we were made for.

The prepositions of the Eucharistic doxology give us the root script for our daily lives: through Christ, with Christ, and in Christ. We were baptized into the profound reality of the Body of Christ. Whenever we send an email, open a book, talk to a friend or a stranger in a store, we do all of it *through* Christ—whether or not we think about it—because we do it as members of his Body. Whenever we make a phone call, read the news, or even turn on the TV, we do all that *with* Christ. After all, the other name given to him, besides Jesus, was "Emmanuel," God-with-us (Matt 1:23). He himself said that "with" is a permanent reality, at least from his side of things: "I am with you always" (Matt 28:20). So unless we walk out of our identity as members of his Body and slam the door behind us, we are always with him. A good bit of our Christian life and growth is discovering what that means. Always, always, always—day and night, for better or for worse, in sickness and in health, for richer or for poorer, we "live and move and have our being" *in* Christ (Acts 17:28).

It really is all in the prepositions. As we pray this doxology silently at Mass or in the depths of our hearts throughout the day, may it become the law of our belief about ourselves and all of our relationships. And may it become the law of our life, a life whose every moment says to Almighty God, "All glory and honor is yours, for ever and ever. Amen."

Star of the Sea

Hail, Star of the Sea,
God's own gentle Mother,
And ever holy Virgin,
Blessed gate of heaven . . .
Keep our life all spotless,
Make our way secure,
Till we find in Jesus,
Joy forevermore.

 —*Ave Maris Stella*

As I write, we are nearing the peak of the Atlantic hurricane season. Storms seem to multiply daily, and we are reminded often of the danger of a wind-roused ocean. As long ago as the ninth century, the seas that ravaged Europe's coasts inspired the hymn *Ave Maris Stella*. The same images appear in the eleventh-century hymn *Alma Redemptoris Mater*, still sung at the end of the Church's Night Prayer in some seasons.

Both hymns lead into an extended prayer for deliverance from sin and evil through Mary's intercession, but they make no further mention of the sea. However, at some point mariners, accustomed to navigating by the stars, picked up the title and adopted Mary, Star of the Sea, as their patron and protector. She remains so down to our day.

The rest of us, safely traveling terra firma on our daily round, might not seem to need the help of such a patron and protector—unless we recognize the perilous sea lapping at every day's doorstep. A wise friend alerted me to it with a warning: "Beware of drowning in a sea of possibilities."

And we can. Consider the invitations flashing on our digital devices: sign up for an online Shakespeare course, download delicious recipes to tickle the taste buds of family and friends, take a virtual tour of St. Peter's Basilica, discover the exercise program we *really* need—or, of course, shop for anything at all! Consider even our parish bulletins: the Bible study group invites us to join, the food pantry is looking for volunteers, we can sign up for adoration day or night. And that's just a small sample, without even looking at our daily to-do lists, the notes on the refrigerator door, the reminders on our phones. Having too many choices is not confined to the electronically savvy or the financially secure. Life circumstances face all people everywhere with a sometimes baffling array of possibilities.

Options are always and everywhere on offer, demanding attention and decision. As the options accumulate, they paralyze. Worse, the recurring possibilities harden into imperatives, creating icebergs floating dangerously in that sea of possibilities. The books you could read become the books you *must* read; the programs you could sign up for become the programs you *have to* sign up for; the meetings you could go to become the meetings you *must at all costs* fit in to an already overcrowded schedule. Drowning is a real possibility.

What to do? Listen to the mariners. Take your eyes off your wet feet (Matt 14:28-31). Look up. Call on Mary, shining steadfastly to guide us. Her light, a faithful reflection of the Light of the World, illumines priorities and dangers, spotlights icebergs before they can crush us, highlights what is most essential for us and our lives versus what comes from someone else's must-have or must-do list. With the mariners and their song, we'll call on her as the gate of heaven, the gate through which Christ's light shines on our storm-battered path and guides us home.

Hail, Star of the Sea! Guide us and those we love to safe shores!

Advent and Christmas

Look to the Light: The First Sunday of Advent

When we reach December days, we find the dark encroaching more and more on daylight as the winter solstice approaches. We turn the lights on earlier in the evening and turn them off later in the morning. There are already homes in our neighborhoods where, refusing the domination of the night, Christmas lights burn brightly, though the nativity of the Light of the World is still three or four weeks away.

An unknown author wrote: "Christians live in the dark with their faces toward the dawn." So Advent is our season. The dark surrounds us here in the northern hemisphere, but we know the dawn lies just ahead. And the dawn has a name: Jesus Christ. In this odd, uncomfortable season of Advent, we live in that uneasy space between *already*—Christ our light was born in the flesh two millennia ago—and *not yet*—Christ, bathed in the light of glory, will come to us again.

When we say we believe in the light coming into the Advent darkness, we are claiming hope as our holy ground. Hope is the gift of this season, but it is an elusive gift. We think we have wrapped it snugly in neat definitions, decorating the packages with Advent wreaths and verses of "O Come, O Come, Emmanuel," only to find that the ribbons have come untied and hope is spilling out all over the place. It takes on different meanings depending on where it falls and pools.

When we attach hope to beautiful Advent images like Isaiah's mountaintop meal where lions and bears and wolves share a peaceful meal with lambs and calves and kid goats

(11:6-9; 65:25), we risk turning it into mere wishful thinking. "That would be nice," we muse, looking up from news headlines that make it clear that the lions, bears, and wolves are still devouring lambs, calves, and kid goats with no sign of ceasing. If we attach our hope to fantasies of a future utopia where all the distressingly dystopian movies turn out to be fiction after all, we drift off into empty daydreaming.

Ads picture happy families gathered around groaning tables laden with the advertisers' products, cooked in the advertisers' new cookware, and served on the advertisers' best china. These commercial fantasies allow us to ignore the families torn apart by quarreling, the empty places at table where teenagers have slipped away into the pain of isolation or addiction, the homeless woman rooting through the dumpster for grocery store throwaways, the family eating free week-old doughnuts out of a paper bag. We can all supply the real-life scenarios that punch holes in our daydream balloons and turn them into bits of shredded rubber.

Hope doesn't just wish for the light. It doesn't just dream about pretty sunrises on some white sand beach. Hope rolls up its sleeves and goes to work. It lights the candles, believing the proverb, "It is better to light one candle than to curse the darkness." Hope works to quiet one family feud (at least for Christmas), to bring one carton of cans to the local food pantry, to find a few better blankets for one homeless shelter, to support one family member through a time of crisis. Hope doesn't *talk* about hope. Hope trusts that the dawn will come one day; meanwhile, it lights another candle in the dark.

Every Sunday of December, we will light one Advent candle and put it on the Advent wreath to affirm our hope. And on Christmas Day, our churches ablaze with candlelight, we will celebrate once again our belief that Christ, who has broken the boundaries of the dark, truly came one memorable night, still lives among us as the oft-unrecognized light that burns through the darkness, and will come again in a burst of flaming glory at the end of time.

But for today, let us just light that first Advent candle. Then let's get to work. There is still a lot of darkness out there that needs those candles to set hope alight in the shadowed corners of the night.

Psalm 46: An Advent Prayer for Quiet

God is for us a refuge and strength . . .
so we shall not fear though the earth should rock,
though the mountains quake to the heart of the sea;
even though its waters rage and foam,
even though the mountains be shaken by its tumult. . . .
The waters of a river give joy to God's city,
the holy place, the abode of the Most High.
God is within her, she cannot be shaken . . .
God puts an end to wars over all the earth;
breaking bows, snapping spears, and burning shields with fire:
"Be still and know that I am God,
exalted over nations, exalted over earth!"

—*Psalm 46:2-4a, 5-6a, 10-11*

Every Advent we hear: This is the season for listening quietly to God's Word. And every Advent we remember: It is also the busiest season of the year. What to do?

Psalm 46 offers a suggestive geography. It pictures an outside world where chaos is imagined as earthquake, tsunami, political mayhem, warfare. But there is also an inner world where God's presence and protective power banish all turmoil. There we can sit quietly and hear ourselves think. The obvious Advent strategy is to find the way into that quiet place within while the holiday-mad world around us is in tumult. A blessing for those who can, but many of us find it nearly impossible. Are we then shut out of the holy season's gift?

Maybe not. What if Advent shifts the strategy? While we prepare to celebrate God's entry into human history as Word-made-human-flesh, perhaps we could reconsider where we might go to hear God's Word in the midst of the season's bedlam. Advent and its Christmas sequel remind us that God's point of entry was never a silent sanctuary, outward or inward. After long, tempestuous years of promise, the Word arrived in a stable in Bethlehem—a town bursting with incomers who were summoned for a census, a murderous dictator hovering in the background. So wouldn't it be appropriate to listen for the Word not just within our own hearts but also in the less-than-quiet world around us? What if we learned to recognize the Word in raucous shoppers, quarrelsome family members, and the homeless people we pass by?

We might rather not. Our own inner sanctuary offers a quiet retreat, but the surrounding babble invites us into the chaos of real human dramas where we often don't know what to do or how to help. Psalm 46 offers a strategy for that, too, but not the one we usually come up with. The psalmist's strategy is: "Be still, drop that heavy fix-it toolbox, and just be there where God is." There we might learn to hear God's ever-creating

Word spoken in the human voices of expectation and despair, joy and suffering, desire and anger.

On the Advent doorstep of the Good News made flesh among us, let us be present, pay attention, listen, and seek to love all those speakers milling everywhere, the welcome and the unwelcome alike. Presence, awareness, listening, and love—God's fix-it toolbox—are far more powerful than the bows, spears, and shields we are prone to take up (Ps 46:10). They are, after all, the tools that Christ, the ultimate Word, brings into the world for our salvation. Let us take them up now, in this season of listening—even if only in hurried snatches—so we may learn to put them to use in doing the gospel's work year-round.

St. Joseph and the Puritans

Puritans don't really belong in the Christmas story, at least not the Puritans we remember from elementary school, where we usually met them at Thanksgiving. I had friendly feelings toward the Puritans because their simple clothes were so easy to draw and color in the obligatory Thanksgiving art projects. And the first Thanksgiving always had a nice feeling about it because, for a change, the new and old inhabitants of the land sat down for a good meal together, at a table decorated with that pretty corn, rather than doing their best to wipe each other out. (Remember, this was elementary school. What did we know about real history?)

Of course, real history does tell us that there were wise Puritans, devoted to God and concerned for their neighbors. But it wasn't till years later, in high school and college, thanks in part to Nathaniel Hawthorne's *The Scarlet Letter*, that I learned something about the repressive downside of some Puritan beliefs. And it was later still that I met the strict Puritan who inhabits my own interior world. Whenever the lifelong call to conversion invites me to break out of whichever particularly restrictive box I've built around myself (and around God), and to breathe the freer air of the Holy Spirit, the Puritan appears on the scene. With lips pursed, nose upturned, and a suitable severity about the eyes, the Puritan warns me sternly: "You mustn't. There are rules, you know, and you must abide by them. Otherwise God will go off and find someone else who is really holy and doesn't think adventuresome thoughts." Of course, the inner Puritan never identifies the actual author of all those rules. Rarely is the author God. It is more likely my mother or my third grade teacher or my novice director or all the rule makers I've met since, including myself.

And I usually fall for it, until God steps in and reminds me of the extraordinarily imaginative and unprecedented work of creation, or Jesus' bad habit of irritating Pharisees by breaking out of their rules in favor of God's rule of love, or the Holy Spirit blowing the first disciples out of the locked safety of the upper room into the street, where God's Word obliged them to be very unconventional indeed. One of the profound and recurring messages of the Scriptures is that God doesn't like boxes. Nor does God like rules that squelch any aspect of our humanity. In fact, God gave and gives us rules for one purpose only: to teach us how to be fully holy by becoming fully human. And those rules God *does* expect us to abide by, and helps us to do so, whatever our inner Puritans think.

Jesus sums up God's rules in the two great commandments of love (Mark 12:28-33) which have always taken holy people out of pious boxes and into the streets, where the redeeming Christ continues to live and walk. St. Teresa of Calcutta, for example. Or St. Thérèse of Lisieux, whose feet never left her cloister but whose desire for a world redeemed took her heart to the far reaches of the earth. Or St. Maximilian Kolbe, who persuaded even Nazi soldiers to set aside their own rules about who must die so that he could take the place of a family man. The list goes on: just add the holy people you admire, canonized or not.

This brings us to St. Joseph. Joseph, says the Gospel, was a righteous man, his righteousness defined by his obedience to God's law (Matt 1:19). That obedience required him to give up his plans to marry his betrothed, Mary, a respectable young woman suddenly found to be pregnant, but not by him. Such a marriage was against the law, as was Mary's presumed infidelity. But already we see the law of love creeping in to undermine the kind of rigid, unreflective obedience that Joseph's inner Puritan, if he had one, would have insisted on. (And no doubt he did have a Puritan or two lingering around, because inner Puritans especially like to take the law-abiding under their tutelage.) Indeed Joseph makes the only concession that the law as he understands it will allow: he decides to divorce Mary quietly (betrothal was considered the first stage of marriage).

We shouldn't get too romantic about this. Marriages were arranged in those days. They were matters of building up families rather than of individuals falling in love. Because we know very little about Joseph except that he was a righteous man and a carpenter, we can't even know how well he knew Mary, given the restrictions regarding unchaperoned conversation between single men and women. His decision to spare Mary the danger of death is not necessarily the act of a man crazy in love in the modern sense. It is the act of a man already clearly governed by God's law of love—that is, of choosing another person's good as the best criterion for action. Of course, this is not to say that Mary and Joseph did not come to love one another deeply after they were married. To be holy means to be loving, so love was certainly the centerpiece of the relationship of this holy couple.

With Joseph's decision made, along comes the angel. In a dream, the angel tells Joseph quite clearly and explicitly to set aside God's familiar law about marriage, to venture out into very new territory indeed, and to marry a woman whose child, apparently illegitimate under the law, is none other than the work of the Holy Spirit. Joseph, dreaming, can't have had a clear theological understanding of what that meant. But what he did have was his own willingness to do as God told him, even if it made no real sense to him at all.

Joseph's inner Puritan must have had a fit. "An angel? How do you know it was an angel? Why would an angel, if it was an angel, bother with the likes of you? Pride, that's what it is! Marry a young woman whose behavior has been questionable, to say the least? Forget about it. The law is the law. Go back to that original plan—already a bit too lenient, I would have thought—and set her aside quietly. None of this venturing out into uncharted seas for you, my man."

Fortunately for the history of the world, Joseph ignored the Puritan. He is surely the patron saint of those whose inner Puritan threatens to suffocate them in a locked box that has no key. Most of us remain unvisited by angels, in dreams or otherwise, but we do get strong prods from the God of love. In fact, when Joseph's story is read at Mass every year on December 20, the next day's *O Antiphon* calls Christ "the key of

David" who opens doors (and maybe boxes) that no one can close.

When Christ opens a door and invites you in, don't let your inner Puritan fool you. Seek a little wise advice from someone who knows how to identify where those inner voices are coming from. Then, if your guide gives you the nod, walk on through that door. Who knows what wonders, what love, might be waiting?

Come, Lord Jesus

"Come, Lord Jesus!"

—*Revelation 22:20*

This short petition peppers our Advent prayers with urgency. In this uneasy season, sandwiched between a long-ago past and a far-distant future, we are rather like small children in the noisy, crowded aisles of a giant store discovering that we are alone amid the holiday lights and too-early Christmas music. We look around desperately and cry out for the One we have lost sight of: "Come, Lord Jesus!"

When we gather for liturgy, with the prophets of old we remember Israel's longing for God to send an emissary, a messiah, one who would rescue them from centuries of oppression. And with all the Church since Christ's ascension, we look forward in hope toward his promised return at the end of time. In this context, the "already and not yet" that characterizes the season seems somehow to suggest that Christ left long ago and will someday return as promised—but he is not here right now. Yet as the nights grow darker, the world's violence becomes more threatening, disease roams everywhere, and hunger is more urgent in nearly every corner of the world, it is right now that we need Christ!

The little petition "Come, Lord Jesus!" is usually used only during Advent, this season of "back then" and "somewhere down the line." But it really is a prayer for right now. We can adopt it amid the chaos of the secular preholiday season and long afterward. Prayed silently or aloud, it is a spontaneous petition we might send Christ-ward in all manner of moments.

When we find ourselves smothered by anxieties, the gift list too long and money too short, let us stop and pray: "Come, Lord Jesus!"

When we find our inner prayer silenced by the noisy demands of the outer world, let us stop and pray: "Come, Lord Jesus!"

When we lose loved ones or a home or a job in this season of hope, let us stop and pray: "Come, Lord Jesus!"

When we find an oasis of peace or a moment of joy in the midst of it all, let us stop and pray, "Come, Lord Jesus!"

Whatever our circumstances, alone or together, in the supermarket or in church, at home or at work, on the road or in an airport or wherever, let us stop and pray: "Come, Lord Jesus!"

The season's unintended impression that we are praying to a Christ long-ago born and long gone until sometime in the future is an illusion. At Christ's ascension, the Acts of the Apostles says that "a cloud took him from their sight" (1:9). It doesn't say he left; it just says they couldn't see him. Although now seated at the right hand of the Father, Christ didn't leave us. He never has. We can't see him in the flesh as they did before his death and resurrection. We don't watch him in action as they did, healing lepers or feeding crowds. But we do sing the old Advent hymn, "Come, O come, Emmanuel." Let us remember that *Emmanuel* is Jesus' other name, revealed by the angel Gabriel announcing his imminent birth to Mary and Joseph (Matt 1:23). And *Emmanuel* means "God-with-us." Still. Always (Matt 28:20).

So when we call him, he doesn't have far to come because he is already here with us. In this season. In every season. In Word, in sacrament, in everyday experiences, he is among us—we are, after all, his Body.

Right this minute, we cry out, "Come, Lord Jesus!" And the answer is always, "I'm right here!"

Glory to God in the Highest

. . . and on earth peace to people of good will.

—*The Roman Missal (see Luke 2:14)*

I n the skies over Bethlehem on that memorable night long ago, the Christmas angels taught us the first two lines of a song we still sing every Sunday, solemnity, and feast day. Over two thousand years and counting—that's a good run for such a simple lyric!

We remember it especially in December, though, because it announces the very first Christmas gift: "on earth peace to people of good will." As the daily news reports another terrorist attack on a busy city street, the current death toll of the war in wherever, the latest school shooting, yet another riot, or one more case of domestic violence, there is no other gift we long for quite so urgently.

Yet the gift doesn't look like much at first. Contemporary Christmas cards notwithstanding, this peace isn't that mountaintop banquet where lion, bear, and wolf sit down for a meal with calf, lamb, and kid goat—the latter trio as table companions rather than menu items (Isa 11:6-9). It isn't even the quiet that follows after spears have been hammered into farm tools (Isa 2:4; Joel 4:10) or nuclear technology is used for medicine rather than weapons. This peace comes before all those things and makes them possible. This peace is a person—a newborn baby, in fact, one of thousands born that night. The gift comes with a name tag: Jesus. That's it. Just Jesus. Angels have to explain that the name means "God will save us" (see Matt 1:21). But how? Sorry, no user's manual provided.

The gift is oddly wrapped too. Where we might look for gold foil and red velvet ribbons to assure us of the gift's worth, all we see are swaddling clothes, bands of ordinary cloth that might cover any poor couple's baby. But God has a long history of wrapping valuable gifts in unpretentiousness: a baby in an Egyptian papyrus basket, a shepherd boy with a slingshot, simple Passover bread just like the bread on supper tables all over Palestine. "Ordinary" is our clue that God, not Santa Claus, has delivered this first Christmas gift.

Ordinary, but oh-so-valuable. Over time the community of believers wrote a thank-you note, quite a long one—the *Gloria* as we now know it. Tucked among the lines praising the gift's giver—our Trinitarian God no less!—is a hidden price tag: "Only Begotten Son." We tend to breeze right by that phrase out of long habit. But think about it: God gave us not a trinket picked up at the local bazaar, not even an impressive warrior king like David, but *God's own and only Son.* This is the One who will become the "Lamb of God" sent to carry away our own sins and dispose of them. That's no ordinary lamb. It's the Paschal Lamb, slain to shield God's beloved people—us—from ultimate death. John's Gospel seems almost to stammer over the explanatory note later attached to the gift: "For God so loved the world . . ." (John 3:16). We could read the amount on the price tag as "priceless"—but it isn't. Not to Father, Son, and Spirit, who paid the bill.

But didn't the angels say that first Christmas gift was "peace"—not a person, never mind *this* person? Yes. But one of the Advent prophets, Micah, says they are one and the same thing: "[H]e shall be peace" (5:4). He who "is our peace" will bring our sorely divided hearts and our wounded world into one on the cross, the final price tag (Eph 2:14-16).

Next Sunday at Mass, when we sing this ancient and perhaps too familiar hymn, let's remember that first Christmas gift and what it really was and is. Our thank-yous—"We praise you, we bless you, we adore you"—may not sound particularly angelic, but our hearts will carry the tune with conviction before the God whose love has more than earned our grateful thanks.

Psalm 1: A Baptismal Prayer for a New Year and a New Start

Blessed indeed are those
who follow not the counsel of the wicked,
nor stand in the path with sinners,
nor abide in the company of scorners,
but whose delight is the law of the LORD,
and who ponder God's law day and night.

Such people are like trees that are planted
beside the flowing waters,
that yield their fruit in due season,
and whose leaves shall never fade;
and all that they do shall prosper.

Not so are the wicked, not so!
for they, like winnowed chaff,
shall be driven away by the wind.

    —Psalm 1:1-4

Who doesn't love a fresh start? New Year, new calendar page, new possibilities.

By a happy intersection of civil and liturgical calendars, January brings us the feast of Christ's baptism, foundation and reminder of our own. Baptism is the greatest of all fresh starts: the old self with all its twists and shadows is washed away, the new self is born from the waters. For the baptized, a gift to live from; for those preparing for baptism, a gift to live into.

But Jesus' own story warns us that a new start is only that: a start. The question every new beginning asks is: What now? As Jesus emerged from the Jordan, he heard God's voice call him "my beloved Son" (Mark 1:11). But very soon, he heard another voice, this one in the desert, offering to rewrite "Son of God" into the story of an immediate, rousing success with no fuss, no muss, and certainly no crucifixion. The price? Stop listening to God's voice and listen instead to the Tempter's. (Genuine listening, remember, always translates into obedience. See *The Rule of St. Benedict*; Prologue 1–2.)

As we begin a new year and celebrate Christ's baptism and our own, we rediscover that Jesus' story is also ours. The psalm that begins the entire psalter spells out the choice we have to make, not just once but day after day as the year unfolds: Listen deeply to God's law, the law of love embodied in Christ and spelled out in the Gospels. Or listen to those other voices clamoring countless variations on the Tempter's invitation to take the quick and easy road unburdened by the invitation and promise of the cross. The psalmist adds a poetic picture of both stories' endings: a tree that offers shade and fruit to all comers, or empty husks that feed no one before blowing away in the wind. We're the listeners. We get to choose.

A New Year's postscript: If next week, or six months from now, we find ourselves still succumbing to the Tempter's many voices, let's ask for the strength to block our ears to the whispers of discouragement that inevitably follow and hear instead God's words of encouragement: "The Lord's acts of mercy are not exhausted, / his compassion is not spent; / They are renewed each morning" (Lam 3:22-23). By nature of our baptism, we are "God's children" (1 John 3:2). In Christ, we are the beloved of God.

Listen!

**Lent and
Easter**

Ash Wednesday: Opening Prayer

Grant, O Lord, that we may begin with holy fasting
this campaign of Christian service,
so that, as we take up battle against spiritual evils,
we may be armed with weapons of self-restraint.

—*The Roman Missal, Collect for Ash Wednesday*

In a world engaged in wars hot and cold for more years than most of us can remember—and in a world of horrific acts of violence off the battlefields—the words *campaign, battle, armed,* and *weapons* conjure up pictures far more disturbing than our usual Lenten talk about *desert, journey,* and *conversion.* The language of spiritual warfare is at least as old as Ephesians 6:10-17. It reappears in many spiritual classics. Yet the Ash Wednesday call to take up arms and go to war is jarring to the modern ear.

But it calls us to a war like none we've ever seen. The leading adversaries are not geographical, political, or economic. They are Jesus Christ and the devil, as we hear in the Gospel: ultimate good versus ultimate evil (Mark 1:12-13). And we are not simply an audience watching on TV. We are the combatants called to choose sides and pick up our weapons.

And very odd weapons they are: not WMDs or riot gear but "the weapons of self-restraint." Lenten tradition names them as fasting, almsgiving, and prayer. They hint at where the battlefield will be: not on foreign soil, not on the streets of our cities, but in our own hearts. The enemy is not out there somewhere, preferably thousands of miles away. The enemy is at work within us, building all those comforting bulwarks against the one great command: love God with all you've got and your neighbor as yourself (Matt 22:34-40). "Oh, of course we will," we say, "one of these days! But first we'd better stock the refrigerator and add spring clothes to the wardrobe and delete all those demanding or annoying or guilt-inducing people from our contact list. Oh, and get a little rest."

Ash Wednesday announces starkly: "One of these days" is now. Here is our code of conduct, and here are our battle plans—here in the Scripture readings given to us each day at Mass during Lent. Here we will find instructions for building and wielding those weapons of self-restraint. A warning: They require no massive budget, but they impose steep costs on those who employ them, demanding as they do the surrender of self-preoccupation and self-satisfaction. They harm no one, but they are painful to those who wield them as these God-given pruning shears get to work (John 15:1-3). They need no boot camps, but they do take a lot of practice, usually a lifetime. And there are no medals, as Jesus warns in the Gospel for Ash Wednesday (Matt 6:1-6, 16-18).

But we do not fight alone. As we dig into the Lenten trenches, we are drawn into communion with our leader, Jesus Christ (Heb 2:10). His ultimate victory over the sin and evil that imprison God's beloved people was won not by violence but by love—a love that led him to lay down his own life so that everyone on all sides of our conflicts will be brought not to death but to everlasting life. Lenten warfare embeds us more and more deeply in Jesus Christ and his story as we travel toward Holy Week and Easter. Then we will celebrate his death, which was not defeat but victory, and his resurrection, which is the only reward that is ultimately worth fighting for—not for ourselves alone but for all our brothers and sisters everywhere. Lent is, as the Ash Wednesday prayer says, the ultimate campaign of service. And we are all in it together.

On Not Wanting to Wake Up

The little noisemaker beside the bed explodes into sound. *Wake up! Wake up! Wake up!* the buzzer calls happily. Or the newscaster announces with professional cheer, "Good morning! Tragedy in the Mile High City! Five thousand people have died in the eruption of an undetected volcano in downtown Denver! Six thousand survivors are suffering from a life-threatening allergy to lava! Five feet of snow have fallen outside your door overnight! Have a good one!" The absence of the aroma of fresh coffee tells you that you forgot to put water in the coffeemaker last night. My ordinary response to such intrusions is to hit the snooze button and go back to sleep. Maybe the day will look better later.

Early in Lent, St. Paul plays the role of alarm clock: "[Y]ou know the time; it is the hour now for you to awake from sleep. For our salvation is nearer now than when we first believed; the night is advanced, the day is at hand" (Rom 13:11-12). The language is more elegant, but the message is the same: *Wake up, it's getting late, there is work to be done!* The temptation to go back to sleep is also the same: maybe life will look better later.

Lent is a serious confrontation with reality. On Ash Wednesday, the ritual blessing and imposition of ashes tells us a truth most of us would prefer to forget: "You are dust, and to dust you shall return" (see Gen 3:19). You are mortal, and the grave awaits you. The reason is spelled out in the verses that precede this one in Genesis 3. Human beings, dazzled by the prospect of becoming "like gods" (v. 5), suffered a tragic loss of memory. Forgetting they were already created in the very image and likeness of the only God there is (1:26-27), they reached out to pluck and eat the magic passport that would carry them into godlike immortality by an easy shortcut. Picture them in fig leaves though we may, set them in an imagined paradise though we will, romanticize them as the innocent victims of the wily serpent though we might, we recognize them all too clearly. They are us, looking for the quick way out of the hard life's work required of us if we would return to the God-likeness that is the birthright we have sold over and over again for a bite of apple or a fast meal of pottage (Gen 25:29-34). If we enter into Lent, we cannot easily escape their story, or our own.

We can, of course, simply close the book and refuse to read. Lent is an offer we can choose to ignore. We can walk out of church, go home to breakfast, wash the ashes from our fore-heads, and forget the whole thing till it's time to go collect palms on Palm Sunday. We can shut the pages of our lives to further scrutiny, lock our self-awareness away in a strongbox, and become Scarlett O'Hara at her best: "Tomorrow is another day!" Yes, it is. So is the day after, and so is the day after that. But whether or not we ever open the book, the story it contains is moving on inexorably toward its conclusion.

Indeed the last chapters have already been written, and we are invited to read one of them during Lent. It opens with Jesus in the ruined garden, now a desert, facing down the serpent who so blinded the first humans to their own truth—and God's. It spells out the right answer to the questions they did not even hear asked: "God is God, and you are not." It paints the portrait of a new humanity enfleshed in Jesus. This human-ity—assumed, permeated, and possessed by the God of love—gives no thought to his own life but only to the lives of others. He writes in the story of his own days and nights the tale of humanity as it could have been and could still be: he loves, he teaches, he prays, he loves, he feeds, he forgives, he heals, he loves. That is the story we were meant to live, had the first chapters not gone so dreadfully awry. That is the story we are asked to rejoin in progress right this very minute, now during this very Lent, by learning a different way of seeing ourselves, one another, God, and the world around us—by acquiring a different way of thinking about life and living it, and by finding a different way of dying than the one we so often seem to choose by the way we live.

Yes, the next-to-last chapter of the story still brings us to death. Lent does not allow us to imagine that our mortality has somehow evaporated overnight. It has not evaporated, but it has been transformed. The story does not end with the sealing of the tomb as the Mother and the other women, with Joseph of Arimathea and Nicodemus, stand grieving at the final thud of the stone (Luke 23:50-56). It ends, rather, with the stone rolled back, the tomb empty, the sun rising out of the dark night, the women rejoicing even in their confusion because their dead Savior lives—and with him, all of us (Matt 28:1-10). Deeply bewildered, the disciples find him walking along the road (Luke 24:13-35), they touch his open wounds (John 20:19-29), they eat his bread (John 21:13), and finally they watch him taken up into heaven (Luke 24:51). The curtain falls. But that is not really the end either. There is a long epilogue—centuries long in fact—where the gospel is preached and lived, men and women are baptized into Christ, humanity struggles to find its way out of the dark clouds and into the light that cannot be extinguished (John 1:5). The final ending will be the ultimate victory of life over death, but that ending is shrouded in obscurities we have not yet learned to read.

That is the real last chapter, but whether it will be *our* last chapter is up to us. Lent is an opportunity to sit down and do some serious reading in the book of our lives thus far. It is also an opportunity to rewrite the parts that lead nowhere, unless nowhere is the destination we prefer. Lent is a chance to plot a new ending. It is a time for listening, for reflecting, for praying, for taking part in God's work of transforming our lives, for practicing the one essential discipline of loving others more than we love ourselves. It is a time to discover once more, perhaps to our surprise, that all this Lenten work is in fact a source of joyous freedom, not a chore at all.

We can do all this and more if we choose to accept St. Paul's wake-up call: "[T]he night is advanced, the day is at hand. Let us then throw off the works of darkness [and] put on the armor of light; let us conduct ourselves properly as in the day, not in orgies and drunkenness, not in promiscuity and licentiousness, not in rivalry and jealousy. But put on the Lord Jesus Christ, and make no provision for the desires of the flesh" (Rom 13:12-14).

Or we can go back to sleep. Every Lent—every day—the choice is ours.

A personal note, in case you were wondering: Since I became a contemplative Benedictine nun, I have awakened to the sound of a bell, not a clock radio! And there is no snooze button!

On Becoming a Blessing

The world is charged with the grandeur of God," wrote Jesuit poet Gerard Manley Hopkins. After painting a bleak picture of all that human beings have done to seal the surface of life against the eruption of God's grandeur, the poet refuses despair, saying:

> There lives the dearest freshness deep down things;
> And though the last lights off the black West went
> Oh, morning, at the brown brink eastward, springs—
> Because the Holy Ghost over the bent
> World broods with warm breast and with ah! bright wings.

Beneath our Lenten ashes, we live in hope of Easter morning when life will spring into new freshness through the power of the Spirit.

Lenten hope is no pipe dream. It is realism with its sleeves rolled up, eager to do whatever is necessary to release the outburst of life promised in Christ. The world *is* charged with the grandeur of God. The Holy Spirit unleashed through the death and resurrection of Jesus broods and bubbles with life at the heart of things. Blessing is what happens when that holy ferment is released into our consciousness. We become aware of God at work within and through the world, and we awaken that awareness in those who participate in the season's rites of blessing—from the blessing of ashes to the blessing of fire, from the blessing of catechumens with the Sign of the Cross to the blessing of the baptismal waters. These blessings are a firm statement of our belief that the hidden grandeur of God "will flame out, like shining from shook foil" (Hopkins), as the fire of the Spirit burns through the caked and trodden surfaces that conceal it. This is the fire Jesus came to cast upon the earth (Luke 12:49).

Abraham and Sarah are figures of Lenten blessing. God made them an impossible promise of life: "I will make of you a great nation, and I will bless you; I will make your name great, so that you will be a blessing" (Gen 12:2). What made the promise seem impossible was that the couple was elderly and childless. They were unlikely candidates to receive and pour out God's abundant blessings on the world through a great nation of descendants "as countless as the stars of the sky and the sands of the seashore" (Gen 22:17). Yet receive it and pour it out they did.

People of trust and conviction, like Abraham and Sarah, continue to be the ones through whom blessing flows into the world around us. Perhaps we see them most dramatically in moments of tragedy. The mettle of Abraham's faith was made manifest in his unquestioning willingness to obey God's startling command that he sacrifice the very child God had given to fulfill the promise of descendants (Gen 22:1-19).

Not all the participants in history's dramas are granted the last-minute reprieve given to Abraham's son. Twentieth-century German philosopher Edith Stein was compelled by her search for truth to embrace Christianity. In so doing, she cut herself off from both the faith of her observant Jewish family and the atheism she shared with respected professional colleagues. Her deep appreciation for the cross led her to take the further step of becoming a Carmelite nun, taking the name Sister Teresa Benedicta of the Cross, thus turning her back on whatever acclaim she might have garnered from a brilliant academic career. However, she never abandoned her love for her Jewish roots. Offering her life for her fellow Jews in communion with the crucified Christ, she was herself arrested and put to death in Auschwitz (1942). She made no attempt to avoid the cost of her choices. Rather, she treasured it.

On September 11, 2001, Father Mychal Judge, OFM, of the New York City Fire Department, went into the burning North Tower of the World Trade Center to minister to victims and died there. The photo of his fellow firefighters carrying his body from the rubble has become a modern icon of fidelity even to the point of death.

Abraham and Sarah, Edith Stein and Father Mychal have all been blessings, awakeners to grace. And their company is legion, as every disaster reveals, whether it be a tsunami drowning vast tracts of Indonesia, a hurricane washing away much of New Orleans or Galveston, or infernos swallowing towns, fields, and forests in our western states or on the continent of Australia. Out of every disaster come men and women by the score to hand on the blessings they have received and awaken us to the grace they have come to know, often through their own willing suffering.

We need not wait for tragedy to discover God at work, blessing us through those around us. Abraham, Sarah, Edith Stein, and Father Mychal responded to tragic circumstances out of the choices of a lifetime, just as Jesus himself did. Lent is the season of winnowing: we sort out the choices we have made, discarding those that have led to deadness of spirit, reinforcing those that have led to deeper life.

In this process, too, we help one another. A friend who perseveres in the long, painful process of recovery from addiction sustains me in my own struggle to be faithful to the Lenten work of conversion of mindset and habits. Someone who has enjoyed public success in politics or sports but chooses to abandon it for the sake of family life or service to others prods me to question my own patterns of self-seeking. A coworker who quits because the expectations of the job cannot be reconciled with gospel ethics forces me to consider my own compromises.

These human "blessings" may be candidates who are as unlikely for the role as Abraham and Sarah. Like Abraham who lied (Gen 20:2) and Sarah who laughed (Gen 18:12), like Edith Stein and Father Mychal who are too recently remembered to have been cast in plaster yet, they are not perfect. Almost every hero and heroine of Scripture had clay feet. But all of us, in our ordinary fallibility and our daily lives of grace, are blessings to one another whenever the God at work in us shines through, if only for a moment—"like shining from shook foil"—to awaken the world to the grandeur with which it is charged.

The Wisdom of the Moths

One morning, intending to leave my office to run an errand, I opened the door only to find my way barred by one of our community's first-year candidates on a ladder. "Oh no!" I thought. "The revolution has begun! They're on the barricades! We're under siege!" (One never knows with newcomers. Remember Maria in *The Sound of Music*!) In reality, she had climbed up there to clean the dusty corpses of moths out of the light fixture over the door.

Poor moths! They never learn. They die by the thousands in light fixtures all over the house, impelled by what Percy Bysshe Shelley (1792–1822) described in lines from the poem "To—":

> The desire of the moth for the star,
> Of the night for the morrow,
> The devotion to something afar
> From the sphere of our sorrow . . .

I wonder, though, if the moths are not wiser than we. They perish in the realization of their greatest desire: communion with the light.

At Matins (early morning prayer) we recently read the passage from Exodus where Moses—attracted by the strange sight of a bush that burns unconsumed—swallows the bait, goes over to take a closer look, and finds himself with a whole new, unexpected, frightening life on his hands (Exod 3:1-10). Moses is one of the moths: from that moment on, he is plunged into God's "burning *yes*"—*yes* to the hard work of liberating God's people from slavery despite their own fears. This work consumes Moses' life until he dies a very old man on Mount Nebo, looking out over the Promised Land (Deut 34:1-6). Although Moses had some acrimonious arguments with God about the whole thing along the way, he seems to have considered the land worth the burning. In contemporary language, we might say that he died fulfilled.

The story reminds me of another often-quoted stanza, this one by Elizabeth Barrett Browning (1806–1861):

. . . Earth's crammed with heaven,
And every common bush afire with God;
But only he who sees, takes off his shoes,
The rest sit round it and pluck blackberries . . .

Back at our own burning bushes, sitting 'round the bush plucking blackberries is certainly safer than hurling oneself into the fire. You get light, warmth, and a tasty snack. Nothing else changes.

But doesn't discipleship always impel us into the flames? Doesn't it mean that we have something (or Someone) we believe is worth burning *for*? Doesn't this way of life draw us into communion with the One in whom the fire of God burns the brightest? Stephen R. Covey writes of the "burning *yes*" that enables us to say "no" to all the lesser invitations that can clutter our days into purposeless chaos. To have a dream worth living and dying for is the stuff of greatness. For Christians, it's the pull of the cross, that narrow gate that opens out into Christ himself (Matt 7:13-14). There we will find a quality of life and love of which we have hardly dared to dream.

In biblical terms, the fiery presence of God in our midst, first made known to Moses at Horeb in the burning bush, is often called God's "glory." We see the term again and again in both the Old Testament and the New. In John's Gospel, Jesus says: "I wish that where I am they also may be with me, that they may see my glory" (17:24). See it, yes—and share it: "I have given them the glory you gave me" (17:22).

To share in Jesus' glory is to leap (or fly) into the fire. It is to become a part of Jesus' "burning *yes.*" Like the moths, we will perish, but what perishes is not our true selves but the all-ruling ego to which we are enslaved—as enslaved as the Hebrews were to Pharaoh. Out of those ashes, the phoenix rises. In Christ burning with the presence of God, our true selves only burn greener and brighter, like that astonishing bush.

The moths seem to think the hall light is worth perishing for, though it's only a bit of plastic they've mistaken for a star. A good bucket of Browning's blackberries will earn us that pale sort of imitation "glory." Fortunately for us, Jesus makes impassioned efforts to convince us that such a gain as that is *not* worth the loss: "What profit would there be for one to gain the whole world and forfeit [one's] life?" (Matt 16:26).

He does not lie to us. Like the moths, we will find that the fire we so long for hurts. Our falsities do not die quietly or painlessly. Still, I think somehow the moths have it right. The yearning for a star worth the time, the effort, and even the sacrifice of those easy-to-pluck blackberries is built into us, as the desire for communion with the light is built into them.

Lent seems a good time to stop and check that it's not just the hall light we're headed for. During the Easter Vigil, the *Exsultet* sings of Christ, the Morning Star, the true Light that the human heart desires. Christ, the Light of the World, offers us no mere plastic surface, here today and gone to recycling tomorrow. Christ offers us instead the radiant reign of God, where there will be no need for hall lights or lamps of any kind—*God* will be the light (Rev 21:23; 22:5). And that light will draw each of us in unique ways, depending on each one's story, call, personality, experience. There may be only one light, but it shines through many windows, as the one sun shines through the glorious windows of the great cathedrals as well as the smudged and broken windows of the poorest hovels.

And in every case, as the moths seem to know, communion with the Light is worth the burning.

Strength for the Cross

When we were kids, we learned to divide the world into people who were stronger than we were and people who were weaker. "Stronger" meant people who could make us do what they wanted, usually because they were taller, heavier, faster with their fists, or they physically outclassed us: the play-ground bully, the big kids, even adults. "Weaker" meant people who had to do what *we* wanted: littler kids. As life got more complicated and we learned the ropes of emotional and moral power, the categories expanded to include the ones who didn't cry vs. the ones who did, the smarter kids vs. the not-so-smart, the ones who could manipulate vs. the ones who could be ma-nipulated, and so on. But the basic criterion for judging re-mained the same: the ones who had the power were the ones who won. In a world where surviving and thriving matter, we learned to admire strength because it was the mark of those who succeeded in one way or another.

As an awareness of suffering and death began to color our world, we added a new dimension to our picture of strength as a quality to be admired and desired. The people next door lost three children in a hideous school bus accident; they grieved their loss deeply—and then continued to make a warm and loving home for their other children and an aging grandparent. A gifted musician at our church had a stroke that paralyzed one hand—and devoted all that creative energy to teaching music at a local rehabilitation program for other stroke survivors. We caught glimpses of the true greatness of the human spirit and saw in it a star we wanted to reach for.

The Beatitudes set out in Matthew 5:1-12 paint a picture of strength both as power and as endurance, but they give it that odd gospel twist that sets all ordinary ideas of what is good on their head, feet waving in the air, as they feel for a new vi-sion of the world to stand on. In the daily arena, there are plenty of ads for life's "power tools"—fitness, health, beauty, savvy, money, top jobs—but very few for the tools of endur-ance—courage, integrity, selflessness—and fewer still for such things as poverty of spirit, meekness, and mercy.

Yet the Beatitudes hint at the strength we see in Jesus. In him there is strength that takes both power and endurance to a level we can hardly imagine. When we hear him speak of the Son of Man coming in the future in glory, riding on the clouds and surrounded by his saints (Matt 24:30-31; 1 Thess 4:14-16), we see the same powerful figure the author of Revelation had in mind when speaking of the "King of kings and Lord of lords," riding at the head of an army that will smash the forces of evil (Rev 19:11-16). Yet during Jesus' lifetime, we see instead one who laid aside all the power and privilege of his messiahship and divinity to put his life and his death at the service of human redemption. Not once does he call upon superhuman forces—his own or the "legions of angels" at his Father's disposal (Matt 26:53)—to spare himself or to make others do what he wants. When his enemies have him arrested, tried, and tortured, he goes unarmed into the pit of hell that human beings devise for one another. He *chooses* to put their good before his own by refusing to subject them to any kind of violence—physical or mental—to make his own lot easier. Even more, he *chooses* to love them throughout the whole horrible process, although they come up with every imaginable way of inducing him to hate them. At the end, he says, "Father, forgive them, they know not what they do" (Luke 23:34). In so doing, he proves himself stronger than all the combined forces of hatred, sin, and death. His is a power and an endurance woven like a seamless garment into one single strength: the love that redefines what it means to be strong.

The Donkey's Story: Palm Sunday

Many years ago, long before I became a Benedictine and learned to treasure our tradition of *lectio divina* (prayerful reading and pondering of Scripture), I learned the Ignatian method of meditation. Since I had grown up in an inner world rich in imagination, the part that most appealed to me was the "composition of place": imagining the scene of whatever biblical story the day set before me, and then imagining myself into the story by "becoming" any character in the scene. This always came quite naturally to me—I had imagined myself into a wide array of cowboy stories and fairy tales and adventure sagas that I heard or read as a child. I carried stories in my head wherever I went, much to the dismay of some of my teachers.

However, when I became a new religious-sister-in-the-making, I tried to be suitably restrained, focusing on the holy people in the Gospel scenes and following the scripts they lived by. I didn't think my formation directors would approve of my identifying with the star in the sky over Bethlehem, reporting on what lay below (and what an interesting report it would have been!), or one of the lilies of the field arrayed in scarlet and gold and smelling like my favorite lilies of the valley (I was still adjusting to an all-black wardrobe).

But I am older now. I don't use this method of prayer as such very often, but sometimes I still indulge in some inner storytelling based on the Scriptures. One day I was thinking about the parable of the Good Samaritan (Luke 10:29-37)—a passage well-worn and even worn out by years of reading commentaries, hearing homilies, and pondering from every possible angle (and even some that are impossible!). Having just about ex-hausted the imaginative possibilities of the poor man beaten and left for dead by robbers, the passing priest and Levite, and the admirable Samaritan himself, I began to notice the other characters in the story—the secondary players no one ever talks about. There were the villains and the innkeeper, of course, but my wayward imagination turned to an even less likely character: the Samaritan's donkey.

Donkeys were very much a part of Jesus' world. They were your everyday beasts of burden, much more down to earth than the exotic camels who fared better in the desert than in town. When Jesus speaks about the gate too narrow to carry all our bits and pieces through (Matt 7:13-14; 19:23-25), he mentions no donkeys, but I often conjure up a picture of one with fat panniers that simply will not fit through that gate, leaving the owner in a painful pickle. When Jesus argues with a synagogue leader about healing on the Sabbath, he turns to the common example of a thirsty ox or donkey (Luke 13:15)—no one would leave it with tongue hanging out till the next day, poor thing! And what Christmas meditation would be com-plete without the donkeys? There's the one we always assume Mary rode to Bethlehem (it would have been a long walk for a pregnant woman). And of course there is often a donkey present and accounted for in our nativity scenes, despite the fact that the Gospels make no mention of one. (Interestingly, the Christian imagination seems to have borrowed the "ox and ass" that we often picture at the birth of Jesus from God's lament in Isaiah 1:2-3: "Sons have I raised and reared, / but they have rebelled against me! / An ox knows its owner, and an ass, its master's manger; / But Israel does not know, / my people has not understood." In the stable these animals stand in mute counterpoint to God's own children, who "have rebelled against" God! So "ox and ass" are a theological comment on the birth of Christ. If only they could tell their story!)

In the parable of the Good Samaritan, the donkey is a willing, silent partner in the Samaritan's work of mercy. Those of us whose daily lives don't bring us into much contact with working animals might think that a common beast of burden had no choice but to collaborate with the owner's plan, but this isn't so. Surely you have seen, as I have, pictures of an overloaded donkey solving its problem by sitting down splat in the middle of the road and refusing to move. And there is nothing quite as immovable as a donkey that has made a single-minded decision to quit! The owner's whip, the driver's cudgel, the air blue with curses—all fail to move the beast. Without bothering with words, it announces, "As soon as you lighten the load, I'll get up. Till then, good luck!" The Samaritan's donkey must have already been carrying saddle bags for its owner's trip, and perhaps it also bore some of his trade goods or purchases. Although we can hope he lightened the load a bit before heaving a man who was all dead weight onto the creature's back, the burden could hardly have been light. But the donkey went along with the plan, willingly doing what needed to be done.

We've all met the Samaritan's donkey—in other guises of course. Every household, every neighborhood, every workplace has bearers of burdens who shoulder whatever load the situation requires of them, unprotesting, unnoticed—and absolutely indispensable. They claim no credit, make no demands for a lighter load, and, more often than not, are undeterred by the fact that no one thinks to thank them. This story calls to mind the load-bearers I live with and makes me grateful to them, sorry to have taken them for granted—and ashamed that I can't claim to be one of them.

So I think rather highly of the Samaritan's donkey, and I hope the Samaritan gave it a big bag of oats once they got to the inn and the victim was unloaded! But I think the real reason it attracted my attention to begin with is that it reminded me of another donkey—one I first met in the era when *The Scarlet*

Pimpernel and *Robin Hood* played regularly across my mind's screen during study period, though I should have been doing my homework. I was probably eleven or twelve when Sister Stanislaus gave us this G. K. Chesterton poem to read:

The Donkey

When fishes flew and forests walked
   And figs grew upon thorn,
Some moment when the moon was blood
   Then surely I was born.

With monstrous head and sickening cry
   And ears like errant wings,
The devil's walking parody
   On all four-footed things.

The tattered outlaw of the earth,
   Of ancient crooked will;
Starve, scourge, deride me: I am dumb,
   I keep my secret still.

Fools! For I also had my hour;
   One far fierce hour and sweet:
There was a shout about my ears,
   And palms before my feet.

Riveted, I've never forgotten the poem, or the donkey. It comes back to me every year on Palm Sunday especially, as I watch in my mind's eye that odd entry into Jerusalem, with the donkey bearing the real Bearer of Burdens. This time it is he, the rider, who is choosing to carry the dead weight of our own sinful, beaten, and broken humanity through the narrow gate into the light beyond, unprotesting, unnoticed by large portions of this world's crowds—and absolutely indispensable.

Behold the Lamb of God: Holy Thursday

Behold the Lamb of God,
behold him who takes away the sins of the world.
Blessed are those called to the supper of the Lamb.

—*The Roman Missal*

The singular depth of this familiar prayer becomes clear on Holy Thursday. By the time we hear this invitation to communion, we will have heard the Paschal Triduum open with the account of the original Passover in Exodus 12. The centerpiece of that event is the lamb sacrificed, its blood sprinkled on the door posts of the Hebrew homes as protection from the Angel of Death, its flesh cooked and consumed at the last supper eaten in Egypt. And we will have remembered another Last Supper, the meal Jesus ate with the disciples before the drama of his own metaphorical passage from Egypt to the Promised Land.

On Holy Thursday, as at every Mass, we remember that for this new paschal feast, it is not our church family gathered around the table who has supplied the lamb of sacrifice. It is God. And we pray to God's Lamb for mercy and peace. Then the presiding priest raises the host and calls us to look, for *this* is that very Lamb of God, here before our eyes. *This* is the One who will protect us from the Angel of Death still roaming our world. *This* is the One who has gathered us together around his table to share this sacrificial meal. *This* is the One who will nourish us, as the first paschal lambs nourished God's people, on the lifelong journey still ahead.

But what we actually *see* seems far too slight to bear all this significance. It is only a fragment made of wheat flour and water, pressed so thin it can be broken with no effort at all. However, as is so often true in the story of salvation, what seems insignificant is in reality world-changing. It has the potential to make any kind of power—even the massed powers of evil, slavery, and death—shake in its boots.

During the unfolding story of Jesus' suffering and death in the Triduum, we discover what a mistake it was to underestimate his power—a mistake made by the political power of Jerusalem's religious leadership and even by the military might of Rome. This Lamb, brought to the table of history by the all-holy God, is the epitome of powerless human misery, mocked, stripped, beaten, nailed to a cross, and left to die. He was surrounded by only a handful of faithful people, mostly women, none of them a threat to anybody.

On Easter, we discover just how big a mistake it was to underestimate him—the utter disaster his passion wrought upon the very forces of evil, slavery, and death. The Lamb returns triumphant from the grave to deliver once and for all those who put such foolish-looking trust in this unlikely Savior.

Let us behold with awe and gratitude—on Holy Thursday, at every Mass, and in the quiet of our hearts—the Lamb of God, given for our deliverance from sin and evil until we step finally into the land where all God's promises will be kept in full.

Tasting Dust: Good Friday

Do you know the taste of dust?

Of course you do. "Remember that you are dust, and to dust you shall return" (*The Roman Missal*; see Gen 3:19). The old Ash Wednesday admonition is echoed in Psalm 103:13-14: "As a father has compassion on his children, / divine compassion is on those who fear the LORD, / who knows of what we are made, / who remembers that we are dust." God never forgets, but we do.

As Genesis 2:4-7 tells our story, God was there, on that riverbank in Eden, right down in the dust, mixing up a batch of clay from earth and river water, and breathing life into it: the first human being! And God still remembers it.

The westerns beloved of my childhood taught me many things about the perennial battle of good vs. evil, though I hardly thought in those terms as a five-year-old entranced by the very first TV cowboys on my grandparents' brand new set. One thing those cowboys taught me was the inescapable connection between dust and death. Many a gunfighter on those shows "licked the dust" or "bit the dust." And I quickly learned that they often didn't get up to rinse out their mouths and go on with life.

Years later, I was a little startled to hear the psalmist express emphatic hope that the enemies of Israel's king would "lick the dust" (Ps 72:9)! But in our stories, it is Jesus himself who licks the dust. We see it happening before our eyes in the Stations of the Cross when we remember him falling down on the dusty road to Calvary, not once but three times. The Gospels don't record those stories, but they are not hard to imagine. Jesus was a fairly young man, muscled by years of toting carpenters' tools and heavy tables and stools. He was further strengthened by an extensive trek the length and breadth of Palestine and beyond. But those travels were incredibly demanding. We can easily see how he might at last have exhausted all his physical resources in preaching, teaching, healing, casting out demons, and even raising the dead. Indeed to "lay down one's life" for all the others means far more than dying (John 15:13). Giving all he had to give, he spent himself utterly in the battle of good vs. evil. And, worn out at last by sleep deprivation, emotional abuse, physical punishment, and blood loss, he fell three times. He got up again each time, the taste of mortality dry as dust in his mouth as he walked on toward that final showdown.

In a very different time and place, and in a very different way, it was the same battle I had learned about when I watched good guys and bad guys fight it out in those long-ago days when you could tell which side a gunslinger was on by the color of his hat. (And yes, they were all men. But I wasn't deceived. I already knew that the fight wasn't limited by gender!) In those old stories, only the bad guys bit the dust for good. If the good guys got shot down, they always got up again, dusted themselves off, and went on their way. So I thought Jesus should too, as he had done on the road to Calvary. Seeing him bite the dust so irrevocably on the cross, I was just sure he would get up again. He had to!

Like Jesus, we all know the taste of dust. We are children of that ancient riverbank, born from dust and destined to return to it. And we too have fallen face down on the road, more times than we can count. And we too have wondered how we will ever find the strength to get back up and journey on.

The answer awaits us on Easter. There we will remember again that Jesus, broken and ground back to dust on Good Friday, did get up again. Transformed and robed in glory, he emerged from the tomb, never to die again.

And, taking the hand he stretches out to us, so will we!

The Silence of the Word: Holy Saturday

Words sting as lies and accusations swarm,
a pestilence of flies, about his head,
released by those who want to see him dead.
Their buzzing horde is thick and black, a storm
cloud gathering to drench the matted hair
in imprecations: "Blasphemy! A god
in dust-stained robes! The roads he trod
all strewn with cloaks and palms! Great David's heir
they hail him! More! He dares address the One
most Holy as his Father! Strike him down!
No regal gems and gold—make thorns his crown!
See what he says to that, this king, this son!"

They wait, but not a single sound is heard.
Death quails before the silence of the Word.

—*Genevieve Glen, OSB*

During Holy Week, we hear: "The Lord GOD has given me / a well-trained tongue, / That I might know how to answer the weary / a word that will waken them" (Isa 50:4). Throughout Jesus' public ministry, we hear him speak again and again a word to the weary to sustain them: "Blessed are the poor in spirit" (Matt 5:3); "Stand up and go; your faith has saved you" (Luke 17:19); "The kingdom of God is at hand" (Mark 1:15). We probably all have a list of our favorites—words that have sustained us, inspired us, impelled us. As the evangelists note, Jesus speaks these words with authority, not simply because he has the prophet's well-trained tongue, but because he himself is the Word of God in human flesh. When he speaks a word of healing, the sick are cured; when he speaks a word of command, demons are driven out; when he speaks a word of forgiveness, the burden of sin is lifted.

We could sit back now and bask in consolation, but Isaiah's prophetic words don't stop there. They continue: "I gave my back to those who beat me, / my cheeks to those who tore out my beard" (Isa 50:6). After Jesus' arrest, his words grow sparse. He limits himself to a few stark statements of the one truth for which he stands, but he does not explain or justify them. Otherwise, to his questioners, his tormentors, his mockers, his executioners, he says nothing at all. He gives himself into their hands without a word of protest or self-defense. Ultimately, he ceases to speak altogether. On the cross, the Word "goes down into the silence," a phrase the psalmist uses for death (see Ps 115:17). What an incredible triumph this seems to be: evil has silenced the Word itself.

Holy Saturday is a day of profound silence. The second reading in today's Office of Readings quotes an ancient homily: "Something strange is happening—there is a great silence on earth today, a great silence and stillness."

I am reminded of the final scene in the film *On the Beach*, when the last human being has been snuffed out by the silent spread of the nuclear fallout from the last world war. In that silence, one hears the flapping of a banner in the wind, the rustle of crumpled papers blowing through the streets, the clanking of a bottle driven against a curb. But one does not hear that one sacred sound: the sound of the human voice, never to be heard again.

The silence of Holy Saturday is not that silence. It is the silence of expectation. We know the end of the story, and we know the final scene is not a sealed and desolate tomb. In that tomb, life stirs. Tradition speaks of Christ's descent into the realm of the dead, where all humanity awaits deliverance. I like to think that in every place where the death of the human spirit has imposed the dreadful wordlessness of despair, Christ the Word has gone before us and awaits us, stirring up new life even as the old life falls quiet. No matter how great our darkness or how deep the silence, Christ has been there before us, and is there with us even now, kindling the spark that can explode into the great fire of Easter. We may not see it; we may not feel its warmth or hear its crackle; but it is there. The silence of death has not snuffed out the human voice forever.

On Holy Saturday night, in all our churches, we will sing peals of "alleluias." They may or may not come from hearts reborn. Life doesn't always follow the Church calendar. There will be people at our Easter services who have tasted the bleak darkness but not yet the light. There will be people whose hearts are keeping vigil with loved ones who are dying even as we proclaim the victory of life. There will be people who know for sure that the tomb is real but aren't so sure about the resurrection. In this liturgical moment, it isn't just the flame of our little candles that we are asked to pass on to one another. Whether we are living Easter or still mourning our Good Fridays, we reach out with the inextinguishable light of Christ to meet one another in the night. "Alleluia" is the cry of faithful people daring to sing aloud into the dark because, once upon a time, a handful of faithful women rushed back from the tomb with the news, "He is not there! He is risen!" And a handful of sorrowing disciples came to believe them.

And to this day, we believers pass on these astounding words, from one person to the next!

The Easter Journey to Emmaus

Where are the alleluias? The two disciples on the road to Emmaus are clearly in no mood for singing as they go. Look at them: shoulders hunched, they walk like old men bearing the burden of a disappointing world. Brows furrowed, eyes on the dust at their feet, thoughts trapped on a dark hill and in a dark tomb, irrevocably sealed in stone. They see no one who will stand at the tomb's entrance and command, "Come out!" (see John 11:43). And so the tomb becomes their own: dead hopes lie there, never to rise again.

It's hardly any wonder these disciples failed to recognize the stranger who joined them on the road (Luke 24:16). They had no room for him in their shrunken and desiccated expectations. And they certainly had no room in their minds to see Jesus as anything more than a mangled corpse wrapped in grave cloths and already returning to dust and bone.

He revived them, of course. They were as hobbled and blinded as Lazarus had been by his shroud, but Jesus spared them the shattering drama of Lazarus's summons from the tomb. Instead, he listened. He knew that once their shroud of discouragement was out in the light where they could name it, he could begin to cut it away and set them free. His blade was the Word of God, "the sword of the Spirit" (Eph 6:17), but he wielded it slowly and gently. Bit by patient bit, he opened the enshrouded eyes of their hearts, using the Word as the psalmist had once described it: "Your word is a lamp for my feet, / and a light for my path" (Ps 119:105). He led them to see the darkness of Calvary from a new perspective opened by that light. Like the good teacher he was, he brought them to the brink of that "Oh!" moment when everything changes. Later they would call the experience fire: "Were not our hearts burning . . . ?" (Luke 24:32).

Perhaps with a hidden smile, Jesus accepted the disciples' urging to stay with them for a meal as evening fell. No doubt Luke, writing decades after the event, took it for granted that conversion from self-centered isolation to communion of love in Christ begins by hearing the Word broken open and then receiving the bread broken and shared. This is the pattern of the Eucharist. And so Jesus first put heart into his down-hearted disciples by giving them new understanding of the Word of God. Then he fed them, strengthened them, and energized them with the bread of his own life.

They were utterly transformed. No more hunched shoulders and downcast eyes, no more hearts weighed down with the burden of dead hopes, no more suffocating burial in their own misery. All that forgotten, they ignored the gathering dusk and immediately ran back to Jerusalem to share the good news with the others whom they had previously left behind. And Jesus, who had disappeared before the meal was over? He went with them unseen, of course. And he still travels with us, so often unrecognized, as we walk that Easter road taken by the two disciples who thought they were just going to Emmaus. And he still feeds us with his own life, wrapped up as Word and bread.

But let's be honest. Our journey is not always a matter of eager alleluias. The road often seems long, and we are tempted now and then to retreat to the apparent peace and security of the tombs we left behind. Clothed though we are with the risen Christ (Gal 3:27), we sometimes cast aside that gorgeous raiment, telling ourselves instead that we're really quite warm and cozy here in the dark, as we shiver in the shroud of self-concern, thin and full of holes, sewn tightly shut with the heavy threads of "should" and "ought" and "can't." What were we thinking? That we were headed toward the Promised Land, and in good company? Disbelief still sneers at us in our idealistic Easter hopes. But don't worry. The risen Christ will come back for us again (John 14:18). And he won't stand outside the tomb of self in which we are confined. He will come in and get us and carry us back out into the sunlight and set us once again on the road, traveling with us as we go. That's what he promised—and he keeps his promises!

Say it with me: *Alleluia!*

Resurrection Step by Step

The book of the Acts of the Apostles, our reading fare at Mass during the Easter season, might well be retitled "The Book of Chaos." It might sell better, chaos being much more a part of our daily experience than apostles are! And it would be accurate. In Acts, Luke chronicles the fascinating ups and downs of the post-Pentecost Christian communities as they spread from Jerusalem to Rome. This is a time of grace, to be sure, but also a time of chaos.

Some of the disciples took with them the memories of the chaos that followed upon the discovery of Jesus' empty tomb in the Gospels. The impression all four evangelists give is that the early Christians were plunged at first into the kind of grief everyone knows from experiences of loss, bereavement, and discouragement, as all their hopes fell to pieces in the wake of the crucifixion. Jesus had certainly talked to them about rising from the dead, but they were obviously utterly unprepared for what that really meant.

How could they be prepared, really? They had an idea of a general resurrection of the dead at the end of time, a belief that had become fairly common among some groups of Jewish believers at that time. The Pharisees, so often painted in dark colors by the evangelists, were prime supporters of that conviction. But vague visions of the far-distant future are a very different thing than having your very dead leader, whom some followers have actually seen sealed into a tomb with a great slab of rock rolled across its entrance, suddenly appear among you, talking to you, sharing food with you, and showing you the very real wounds of his crucifixion. Quite understandably, chaos reigned as people ran around telling excited stories of what they had seen or what rumors they had heard and who had said what and who believed whom—or didn't. Anyone who has ever tried to turn all those accounts into a coherent timeline knows it can't be done because experiences differed so widely.

Amid this narrative chaos, though, there is a single strand that draws all the stories together: Jesus' actual appearances to one person after another, one small group after another, on Easter day and for some time after that. These meetings become pools of quiet, intense conversation with no outsiders there to cause ructions as Jesus gradually convinces all of them that he was indeed crucified, he had indeed died, and he had most certainly risen from the dead and was very much alive. Most importantly, he assured them that he would continue to be with them through whatever would come. "Peace be with you," was the refrain with which he reassured them in their frazzled, frightened confusion (Luke 24:36; John 20:19, 21, 26). And the chaos could never drown that peace.

However, at the end of the Gospels and the beginning of Acts, Jesus has withdrawn from the disciples' sight (Acts 1:9). The Holy Spirit falls upon them and blows them out into the street to tell the whole world the good news. The chaos begins all over again as the stories of Jesus spread beyond the small group of followers to Jews and Gentiles alike—some interested but uncertain, some immediately convinced to join the disciples, some furiously antagonistic. And in the midst of it all, the disciples themselves discover that what they know about Jesus and his teaching will be challenged over and over again by new experiences: disciples sent to do jail time and released by angels; ethnic groups fighting with one another even in the intimacy of the early Jerusalem community; leaders disagreeing over whether and how to incorporate Gentiles into their tight, faithful Jewish-born community; authorities threatening death; believers in Jerusalem forced to flee to other places where not everyone welcomes them. Issue after issue arises, requiring that they deepen and expand their understanding of what Jesus' message means in places far from Galilean hillsides or the Temple in Jerusalem. How is this message to be lived in alien settings? What does it mean to *be* an alien in the Greco-Roman world, without sacrificing anything essential to their faith? Over and over again, they have to learn what it really means to be a follower of the crucified and risen Christ.

And so do we. It would be so much easier if we could simply travel through Lent to an all-encompassing profession of faith at the Easter Vigil and emerge, whether as new or newly transformed Christians, into the simple clarity of a gospel-driven life. We might envy St. Paul who charged up the Damascus road a fire-breathing warrior against this new Christian stuff, only to find himself knocked to the ground by a great light, blinded, skewered by Christ's words, and turned into an ardent campaigner for the gospel almost overnight (Acts 9:1-22).

That kind of starting over on a brand new page has always appealed to me as "real" Easter conversion. But as my fresh Easter script gets blotted or washed out in spots, when I fall on my face all over again, I realize that even for St. Paul, conversion wasn't actually instantaneous. Faith in Christ was, but figuring out what that meant for daily life took long, hard work. Paul spent *years* after his conversion pondering and praying before he emerged as the great apostle to the Gentiles (Gal 1:17–2:1). And even then, with every new encounter in every new place, with every new community offering new challenges, Paul had to deepen his understanding of the mystery of Christ and figure out how on earth he and others should live it.

The story of the early Church—with all its crisis, chaos, and learning—teaches us that although Jesus rose from the dead very quickly, it takes us much longer to grow into resurrection. Deadening habits, stifling mindsets, and wounded histories all require that, with prayer joining us constantly to Christ, we struggle day by day to find our way out of the tomb and into the new life offered to us.

But remember the strand that linked all the episodes of resurrection chaos in the Gospels: quiet, intense personal conversations with the risen Christ. We would call them prayer, and we will find them in our own lives if we look and listen. Remember, too, that it was Christ who appeared to his followers, not they who sought him out. So we know he is here beside us, waiting for us to notice him so the conversation can begin.

The most consoling words I know about this lifelong process of dying and rising come from the book of Lamentations, product of Jerusalem's misery in the wake of conquest and destruction, its own time of chaos:

> Remembering it over and over,
> my soul is downcast.
> But this I will call to mind;
> therefore I will hope:
>
> The Lord's acts of mercy are not exhausted,
> his compassion is not spent;
> They are renewed each morning—
> great is your faithfulness!
> The Lord is my portion, I tell myself,
> therefore I will hope in him. (3:20-24)

Amen! Alleluia!

Easter Unseen

The hard labor of Lent is unmistakable, but Easter is easy to miss. As we read the Easter stories in the Gospels, we realize that what Jesus' disciples saw at first was . . . nothing they could recognize! The early visitors to the tomb, intent upon the work of proper burial, found no body to bury (Mark 16:1-6). Mary Magdalene met the risen Christ in the garden, but she thought he was the gardener (John 20:1-15). The disciples who had gathered together, puzzling over reports that Jesus was risen, found him suddenly in their midst, but they thought he was a ghost, and they panicked (Luke 24:36-37).

Death we understand. Loss and grief wear familiar faces. Whether we like it or not, we know something about how to suffer. The ascetical death-to-self that Lent demands of us is hard work, but it's no mystery. We know perfectly well what our main forms of selfishness look like. Now and then we may be surprised to see a new face in the portrait gallery of "bits-of-me-that-don't-measure-up-to-gospel-ideals," but generally speaking that portrait bears an obvious kinship to the ones that hang there already.

Yes, death and death-to-self are familiar, recognizable. Resurrection is the stranger. New life comes upon us by surprise. So unfamiliar is it sometimes (and how could something entirely new be anything but unfamiliar?) that we take it for a gardener or a ghost. We walk past the risen Christ at work in our lives and mistake him for the landscaper come to replant the flower bed—like a character in a crime story who overlooks a burglar in a delivery person's uniform—because we're too busy looking for someone more dramatic doing something more extraordinary than Jesus is usually doing in the garden of our days. Or we see him in the room of our hearts, and, terrified, mistake him for an intruder. (Shouldn't he be safely in church—or better yet in heaven—instead of right here in my everyday life, which I thought I had locked up so carefully against the unexpected?) Maybe we even think he's a thief who has come to make off with something or someone we prize more than diamonds, rather than a savior who has come to present us with the pearl of great price. We may not realize that he has just brought this pearl back from the field where it was buried, and at a cost far higher than we ourselves might be willing to pay (Matt 13:45-46).

Perhaps the Easter season is lengthier than Lent because the Mystery takes far longer to absorb than does the work of making space for it. The risen Christ at work in our lives is far too great for us to see, recognize, and understand all at once. The task of the Easter season is to recognize the gifts we have been given—and to accept them graciously, with thanks. They probably won't take the form of angels in dazzling white garments telling us that Jesus has risen from the dead. We already knew that! They are probably much more simply dressed: an awareness that some burden we have been carrying has been lifted from us; the realization that someone with whom we were at odds now lingers to say hello (maybe a little hesitantly, a little awkwardly, but willingly all the same); the discovery that a chore we resented has been transformed into an unspoken act of love. These Easter gifts bear the same message as those angels: Don't look for him in the past, among your dead sins and failings. He is not there; he is risen! He goes before you— and you are risen with him! So leave the past here and follow him on down the road (Matt 28:6-7).

The readings from the book of Acts in the Easter Lectionary are encouraging when we find that road a little confusing, a little frightening, or a little harder work than we thought risen life should be. The early Christians also made some false starts, lost a little headway here and there, and even argued with each other sometimes as they tried to locate the footprints of the One who said he was "the way and the truth and the life" (John 14:6). Even the hero and heroine stories of Acts can't disguise the fallible humanity of the Greek and Hebrew converts quarreling over whose widows were getting the best cut of the Church's charity (Acts 6:1), or the confusion of communities of converts who thought they had the whole gospel message but discover that no one told them about the Holy Spirit (Acts 19:1-6), or the earliest missionaries arguing over whether Gentiles could become Christians without first becoming practicing Jews (Acts 15:1-2).

Whether Easter bursts upon us in a blaze of light as we recognize the features of the Lord we have loved and served in new and unexpected places in our lives, or whether it steals over us slowly and quietly so that we almost fail to notice it, it always comes as an invitation to live differently. As Jesus came to the people of Galilee before anyone knew who he was, so also he comes to us now, long after Easter, bearing the same emphatic message: "This is the time of fulfillment. The kingdom of God is at hand. Repent, and believe in the gospel" (Mark 1:15). *Now* is still and always will be the "day of salvation" (2 Cor 6:2)!

The Divine Mercy: What Mary Knew

As we celebrate Divine Mercy Sunday, let us remember that this mercy was not first made known to the frightened, grieving apostles gathered in the Upper Room on Easter Sunday evening. Long before that, Mary, the Mother of Jesus, knew that mercy first.

She knew the mercy as a word given by an angel—a startling word, a puzzling word, a difficult word, a word that demanded more—and gave more—than she could ever have imagined. What kind of mercy is that? Not ours.

She knew the mercy as a child—a unique child, conceived in her own flesh-and-blood womb by the power of God's Holy Spirit. So profound was the mystery of this child's conceiving that the actual moment when the Spirit "overshadowed" her is cloaked in Gospel silence, where the human imagination cannot and dare not venture. What kind of mercy is that, to be so beyond our knowing? Not ours.

She knew the mercy as a baby born in a stable—unnoticed by anyone except the local women who no doubt came to help her; by shepherds who stumbled in by night, babbling about angels and a savior; and by exotic strangers from far away, looking for a newborn king. What kind of mercy is that, to arrive so hidden? Not ours.

She knew the mercy as a son who loved her and who walked away to carry God's mercy in life-changing words and life-shaking actions to all who did not know it—to the poor, the rich, the sinners, the grieving parents, the lepers, the lamed and blinded and deafened, and to those who knew the law but not the love. What kind of mercy is that, to be given so indiscriminately? Not ours.

She knew the mercy as a body—tortured, mocked, reviled by soldiers, religious leaders, and bloodthirsty spectators—as flesh of her flesh hung torn and bleeding on a cross, as her dead child, laid once more upon her lap. What kind of mercy is that? Not ours.

Mary knew the mercy as fire rising from the dark realm of death to set the world alight with God. She knew the mercy fully then as a gift never before imagined—God's love in the flesh, visiting every corner of human experience for a few short, earthly years, bringing shock and joy and challenge and hope, then descending even into the realm of death, there to release uncounted captives seized by God's great enemy and condemned to darkness, wordlessness, isolation, in a shadow life that must have been unbearable. No dark hidden corner of human living and dying was left unvisited and unhealed by this Love who never counted the cost—the cost to himself, that is. The cost he could not and would not tolerate was the cost that sin had forced *us* to pay. *That* he would remedy at any price. What kind of mercy is that? Definitely not ours. (Who would have the courage?)

Mary knew that mercy by name. She knew him as child and man; she knew him dead and risen. She knew—and turned to hand him on to generations yet unborn. You see, the mercy is never given to be kept, as Mary Magdalene learned at the tomb (John 20:17). Christ, God's mercy, is given to all of us to share and to pass on till the entire world knows him as Mary did—and as we have—from generation to generation.

What kind of mercy is this? God's.

References

The Measure of Love
Albert the Great, "Enarrationes: In Secundam Partem Evang: Lucae (X–XXIV)," in *Opera Omnia*, vol. 23 (Paris: 1895), 673.

God's Vocabulary
Maisie Ward, *Caryll Houselander: That Divine Eccentric* (New York: Sheed and Ward, 1962), 136.

Landscapes of Hope
St. Macarius, *Fifty Spiritual Homilies of St Macarius the Egyptian*, trans. A. J. Mason (New York: Macmillan, 1921), 215.

Us and Them
Robert Frost, *The Poetry of Robert Frost*, ed. Edward C. Lathem (New York: Holt, Rinehart and Winston, 1969), 33.

Voice and Word
St. Augustine, Sermon 293A: "On the Feast of the Birth of John the Baptist," in the *Patrologia Latina*, ed. Jacques Paul Migne, vol. 38 (Paris:1857–1866), 1328.

St. Benedict, *The Rule of St. Benedict in English*, ed. Timothy Fry, OSB (Collegeville, MN: Liturgical Press, 1981), 15.

Michael Casey, OCSO, *The Road to Eternal Life: Reflections on the Prologue of Benedict's Rule* (Collegeville, MN: Liturgical Press, 2011), 37.

Surely Not I, Lord?
St. Ignatius of Antioch, "Letter to the Romans," in *The Office of Readings According to the Roman Rite*, trans. International Commission on English in the Liturgy (Boston: Daughters of St. Paul, 1983), 1597.

A Different Desert
Robert Alter, *The Five Books of Moses: A Translation with Commentary* (New York: W. W. Norton, 2004), 17.

Seat of Wisdom
Joseph Cardinal Ratzinger, *Introduction to Christianity*, trans. J. R. Foster and Michael J. Miller (San Francisco: Ignatius Press, 1969), 293–301.

On Becoming a Blessing
Gerard Manley Hopkins, *The Poems of Gerard Manley Hopkins*, ed. W. H. Gardner and N. H. MacKenzie (Oxford: Oxford University Press, 1970), 66.

The Wisdom of the Moths
Percy Bysshe Shelley, *The Poetical Works of Shelley*, ed. Newell F. Ford (Boston: Houghton Mifflin, 1974), 418.

Elizabeth Barret Browning, *Aurora Leigh* (Oxford: Oxford University Press, 1993), 246.

Stephen R. Covey, *The 7 Habits of Highly Effective People* (New York: Simon and Schuster, 1989), 159.

The Donkey's Story: Palm Sunday
G. K. Chesterton, *The Collected Works of G. K. Chesterton* (New York: Dodd, Mead, 1961), 308–9.

The Silence of the Word: Holy Saturday
Genevieve Glen, OSB, *Beside the Streams of Babylon* (unpublished collection).

Also by Genevieve Glen, OSB

Sauntering Through Scripture
A Book of Reflections
By Genevieve Glen, OSB

Paperback, 144 pp.
$14.95   978-0-8146-3700-5
eBook $11.99   978-0-8146-3725-8

"This gentle book encourages us to encounter the people and stories of the Bible in our own lives. Glen has a gift for making us see even familiar stories with fresh eyes. As a monastic Glen is immersed in scripture, day in and day out, and this book strikes me as one fruit of that life. Glen invites us all to share in the wisdom she's gleaned."
    —Kathleen Norris, author of *A Cloister Walk*

For more books from *Give Us This Day* and to place an order, visit GUTD.net/Books or call 800-858-5450.

Life-giving Daily Prayer

Give Us This Day is a personal daily prayer book published monthly by Liturgical Press.

For more information or to request a sample copy of *Give Us This Day*, visit GUTD.net or call 888-259-8470.